THE LAST
ORANGE

THE LAST ORANGE

A Lost and Found Memoir

Kisan Upadhaya

iUniverse, Inc.
Bloomington

The Last Orange
A Lost and Found Memoir

iUniverse books may be ordered through booksellers or by contacting:

iUniverse
1663 Liberty Drive
Bloomington, IN 47403
www.iuniverse.com
1-800-Authors (1-800-288-4677)

ISBN: 978-1-4759-4804-2 (sc)
ISBN: 978-1-4759-4806-6 (hc)
ISBN: 978-1-4759-4805-9 (ebk)

Library of Congress Control Number: 2012916331

Printed in the United States of America

iUniverse rev. date: 10/17/2012

CONTENTS

The Last Orange: A Lost and Found Memoir

Prologue

God's purpose throughout the ages has been to create and sustain the heavens and the earth in harmony and us in His image. God is the source of all life. God is love.

But as we look around we see that God's objective is not complete. The earth is not always in harmony with us, His loving image is often marred. Yet God is at work in the world to complete His plan. He explains His purpose, His complete plan, His love in the Bible from Genesis to Revelation.

God has a purpose for each of us. He comes to each of us one by one because each of us has a unique part to play. We do not always understand that part. We do not always recognize Him. We do not always see the events in our lives as having a greater purpose. We do not always see His love.

Here is the story of one life, God's hand in it, and the results of His love. Please look for Him in the events of your life. Ask Him to show you your purpose in His plan.

The Cast of Characters:

Kisan Upadhaya: the narrator and author

Sani (Maya Devi): my biological older sister

Indralal Upadhaya: my biological father

Umoti Devi: my biological mother

Uncle Bal Ram Sharma: my mother's younger brother

Aunt (name unknown): my father's younger sister from Nepalgunj, Nepal

Uncle Salikram Upadhaya: my father's elder brother

Dal Bahadur Chhetri: my mother's second husband

Diwakar Prasai, my best friend from Pre-K on up

Deepak Wagle: my friend from Nepal who connected me with Rajen Singh

Rajen Singh: a high-ranking police officer in Guwahati, Assam

Parnabjyoti Goswami: Superintendent of Police in Guwahati, Assam

Zarir Hussain: news anchor in Guwahati, Assam (Newslive TV)

ACKNOWLEDGMENTS

To Maya Devi, my older sister who took care of me as a child even though she herself was just a young girl. She was my sister, my best friend, and my mother.

To Diwakar Prasai, my true friend in Nepal from pre-K to university, without him I would not have found my biological family.

To Mendies Haven Children's Home in Nepal. Mummy and Daddy. The Mendies took me into their home as their own son and gave me their last name. I was called Kisan Mendies all throughout school. They made it possible for me to come to the U.S.

To Professor Frank and Ellen Starmer who sponsored me so that I could come to the U.S. and attend community college. They are the reason I now live in the U.S. with a wife and two wonderful children.

To Sagar Thapa my college days friend for providing hotel, room and board during all my travels in Nepal.

To Vir Dewan an Australian writer and speaker who published my story in the U.S., Asia, Fiji, and Australia. I thank him for his hard work in getting my story out to the world and for his support.

To Pam Upadhaya, my wife and the love of my life, who has been there for me through thick and thin. She is a true Proverbs 31 wife.

To Nanda Kirati Dewan, a freelance journalist and activist who helped me find my sister. I'd also like to thank the All Assam Gorkha Students' Union (AAGSU) for their support and help throughout my search for lost loved ones.

Editor: Alice Osborn, M.A.
http://aliceosborn.com

Final check by Pam Upadhaya

Graphics Design: David Rayle, M.A.
thankfulvoicepublishing.org

INTRODUCTION

All throughout the Bible we see that God is an all-knowing God. The Lord knows everything—past, present and future. Isa 41:21-24. Did I know what my future held when I was four? No. I did not even know who Jesus was at the time my story begins.

This is a true story of God's grace and mercy in my life, but I did not fully see it that way until later in life. My dad moved to Assam looking for better job. Later mom also moved there. It is where me and my sister were born. At a very young age, I moved with my sister and mother to Nepal, then to India and then back to Nepal again. As young children, my sister and I were abandoned, neglected and rejected by our own parents and our aunt, my father's younger sister. We were then left on the streets of Kathmandu to survive on our own.

The most innocent time in human life is childhood, when you should be loved and cared for; these are the moments when you want to gather precious memories of playtime, relatives, love and learning that will help you on your way to adulthood. However, for my sister and me, the memories of our childhood are filled with hunger, child-slavery, loneliness, and rejection. We were not afraid to die, but afraid to live.

Nonetheless, my story is not just a story of terror and neglect; I want to portray the solid love and bond between my sister and me as we cared for each other as best we could. I want to demonstrate a new emotional bandwidth of what it was like to be street kids. The emotional adversity, hurts, and the physical abuse of my life back then did not stop me from giving up the will to survive since God found me before I found him and He had mercy upon me. As promised by God in 2 Corinthians 12:9, His grace was sufficient for me.

CHAPTER 1
Early Life: My life as street child after being abandoned by my own family

One hot summer morning in 1965 at 6 a.m. in Assam, India, I was born in a small village called Dergaun, Assam.

Assam is located south of the eastern Himalayas and forges the Brahmaputra and Barak river valleys along with the Karbi Anglong and North Cachar hills. Assam is surrounded by six of the other seven sister states: Arunachal Pradesh, Nagaland, Mainpur, Mizoram, Tripura and Meghalaya. These states are connected to the rest of India via a narrow strip in west Bangal called the Silguri Corridor, or in other words, the "Chicken Neck." Assam also shares international borders with Bhutan and Bangaladesh, adding diverse culture and heritage from Southeast Asia. Assam became a part of India after the British occupied the region following the First Anglo-Burmese War of 1824-1826. This state is known for its tea estates, large and old petroleum resources, Assam silk and its rich biodiversity. Many may not know that Assam has successfully conserved the one-horned Indian rhinoceros from near extinction, along with the tiger and numerous species of birds, and it provides one of the last wild habitats for the Asian elephant. The rich wildlife has proved to be a popular destination for tourists wanting to get a glimpse of these rare animals. Once, Assam was known for its Sal tree forests and forest products which have been depleted now. In fact for thousands of years auromere ayurvedic incense has been made by hand rolling each stick of fragrant dough from the fruit of the Manjal tree.

Assam is very green. It receives a lot of rainfall and is full of coconut, palm and banana trees everywhere you look, reminding me of the Garden of Eden. The lush green mountains reflect silver at sunrise and are golden during the sunset. Right beneath the magnificent mountains lay the foothills with all kinds of wild flowers. The landscape of the mountains, foothills and the valley looks as if a smart architect sat down with plans to render this place a paradise.

Yet it was considered a third world country at the time of my birth during the 60s. The harsh and very hot weather and the lack of education contribute to a very primitive lifestyle for so many. Poverty, disease, death, filth, the crippled and sick who lie and beg on the side of the streets display the sorrow of the nation. Less privileged kids beg for food and money, and the looks on their faces reveal that they are seeking Divine deliverance. Little children run among the city dumpsites in search for something to eat. A dog licks the wounds of a restless soul who lies helpless in the streets. Flies lay their eggs in the wounds.

Many children end up in the train station, where some look for jobs and others become vagabonds, crisscrossing the country on its vast and intricate railway network. They live miserably, enduring constant hunger and malnutrition. Their lifestyle exposes them to drug trafficking, organ trade, prostitution and slavery.

The police don't do anything to protect them and many end up getting further abused by the law enforcement. Girls are raped and murdered and these crimes are never reported. Kids go missing never to be found again. If they are lucky enough to endure and survive the phenomenon they find work as rag-pickers, or work in a tea stall as I did later in the chapter. As you can imagine street life can be very unpleasant and risky as these children become vulnerable to drug dealers who coach them to go out and sell drugs on their behalf or else. Some of these kids live in groups among themselves with at least one elder among the bunch who is the strongest and the ring leader. Various different street kids live a gang-style life and other street kids better not cross their paths. Most fights often break out for small bites of food and a few rupees. Yet the bond between or among themselves is very strong and they do share with each other.

My life was straight out of the film *Slumdog Millionaire* in the slums and streets of Kathmandu during the 60s. I was not born in the streets yet I ended up being one of many unfortunate street kids. When you come from a very poor violent and broken home, where else do you go for refuge? Many are even abducted and pushed into begging and some are even forced into the streets by their own parents who aren't able to feed them. Daughters in some situations are prostituted by their own parents for cash in order for the parents to survive. These girls are especially more prone to the symptoms of AIDS. Life is rough and harsh even today in most parts of India and even in Nepal such practices still exist.

As these kids roam the streets of big cities of India such as Delhi, Mumbi, Calcotta, Chennai, or even Guwahati where I am from, they end up marrying another poor street girl with a similar life and no home to live in. They then become homeless adults, to bear children on street corners and raise them on the sidewalks of major cities. Far too often, the cycle repeats itself with their children as these parents who have nowhere to go nor any place to live. The harsh brutality, the lack of education all lead back to the street and their sad, lonely, neglected lives continue on.

My journey in life began in the foothills of beautiful Kahilipara Guwahati, in a small three room tin-roofed house.

I lived there with my mother and my sister. My mother was a housewife who raised two kids as best she could. Dad was hardly home during weekdays since he worked for the state and would come home during weekends only. Without Dad's help, Mom fulfilled the daily obligations of raising us kids and taking care of the animals and farm.

I remember walking barefoot to school few kilometers away from our house. I managed to go to school all day long, but I do not recall learning anything. My parents did not really care whether I went to school or goofed around elsewhere. My daily activity was not of their concern. I remember sitting on the floor while my teacher stood for hours trying to make sense of something that did not make any sense to me. All he had to teach with was a chalkboard, for there were no books available. Homework was to be done on a slate board I carried around to school. I do not recall doing any homework. During the monsoon (rainy season), the ceiling leaked and all the kids including myself became drenched with the water. Summertime was very hot, while winter was bitterly cold. There were no chairs or student seats; we all sat on the mat on the floor for hours until school was over. Yet no kids complained about the situation for that is all we had and knew nothing better. Although my sister and I walked to school together, we did not attend the same school. We did not bring lunches and no lunches were provided. What little we had to eat before school needed to last until we returned home. Most of the time I went to school hungry.

My childhood school

Nearby was the Assam Police Station Battalion #4 in Kahilipara Guwahati, where my father worked as a police officer until he retired. Right past the police station was a big open field where I used to play football (American soccer) as a child.

Standing just five feet tall, my mother had Mongolian features, long hair, and a golden complexion. She was perfectly rounded and had the sparkling black eyes of a dove. The freckles on her face reminded me of the stars in the night sky. A pair of dimples added extra charm.

My mother was married at 16 to my father, Indra Lal Upadhaya, which was not uncommon in their remote Himalayan village in Nepal. My mother gave birth to my older sister when she was 17 and had me three years later in 1965. As I mentioned before she was a housewife who cooked, cleaned and looked after me and my sister along with our dad.

During the time when Dad was at work and my sister and I were at school, my mother usually took the cows and goats into the woods. A few times I told my mama that I did not feel good and that I did not want to go to school. One day I played sick and she took me with her to the woods to feed the cattle. As I was running around and playing, I ran into a robin's nest: "Mama, Mama, look what I have found!" "A baby robin," she replied. I insisted my mother take the baby robin home so that I would have a pet and she agreed. My mother catered to that robin so well I could hardly believe it. She would chew on some corn and beans and feed the robin with her mouth just as a mama robin would have done. The robin was tiny and it could not fly. Slowly it grew older and started to learn how to fly. I had never dreamt my robin would fly away, leaving me behind, but it did.

My father was a police officer in Guwahati's fourth battalion district and worked along the border. He was hardly ever seen in casual clothes; he always wore his green khaki police uniform. He was a very cheerful person, but his long, thick mustache made him look a little mean. He worked at the border area of Assam, and I hardly ever saw him or got to spend quality time with him as a child. But when he came home, he would pick me up, put me on his shoulder, and carry me into the house. Every payday he would buy candies for me and my sister. What little time he spent with me was enough to make me believe that he loved me dearly and I loved him too.

My sister Sani, three years older than I, always wore a red sari, as was common for girls and women. Like many other young girls, she was self-conscious about how she would look. She would put on a red dot on her forehead to add a little cuteness to her features. She was clever and smart as well as pretty. She and I cared for each other a lot. I was closer to her than to my mom and dad. There was nothing I would have not done for my sister if she needed any help. She was not just my sister, but my best friend.

Being a girl in a poor Asian country left her with no choice but to follow in my mother's footsteps and take care of the household work. Sani went to school until about Grade 3 and then helped out at home. She spent a good deal of time in the kitchen with my mother.

As for me, I was a smiling and joyous little boy who had nothing to worry about, for I was the pet in the family when it came to my mother. (My sister was the pet when it came to my father.) I had thought that I had the best family among all my friends in the neighborhood.

I was about four years old when I started noticing my father coming home drunk and beating our dear mother. One gloomy evening as Sani and I were finishing dinner in the kitchen, my dad came home drunk. My mom and dad went into the bedroom Sani and I shared. We could hear him shouting at my mom and beating her. We ran into the bedroom and watched our dad kick our mom on her bosom, grab her by her hair, and bang her head on the wall. Sani started to cry. Neither of us could stop our father. We just watched helplessly as he tortured my mother. The neighbors could not hear the fighting because our small house was situated at the center of my dad's property. We were alone.

My childhood home

I began to cry. Seeing me cry, Mama came toward me to hold me in her arms, but dad pulled her away from me and slapped her in the face again. The fighting went on and on. It was a one-sided fight. Mama did not fight back. My dad was a police officer and knew how to fight hard without hurting his own hands.

In a rush of fury and confusion, I ran toward my dad as he was about to strike her. I caught his right hand and bit him. I watched his hand bleed. I was young and my teeth were just beginning to get strong and sharp. My father turned and slapped me, leaving five finger marks on my cheek that lasted two days. It was first time that my father ever slapped me, but after I had fallen on the floor, the fight was over. I felt like a man who had stopped a war.

I really thought I had a good and happy family until that fight and all the fights that followed. The joy and happiness I once felt in my small family faded away. Mama was no longer the same cheerful person she had been. Daddy looked hazardous and mean whenever he was home. Sani who had started to bloom as a lotus flower lost her smile and appeared pale as the days went by.

My dad started to live with other women (at least that is what I thought at the time). When he came home to us the physical and emotional abuse was a great burden for my mother. "I can't take this anymore," my mother said. Not just once or twice—it was constant battle every weekend. Should she leave and abandon the children or face ill treatment? Deep in her heart lived a silent wound. Perhaps it was her passion for her kids that kept her going as she weathered the punches.

My mama's life was marked by sadness, sorrow and discontent. She was not educated, could not read or write, was poor, and could not afford to take care of us on her own. My mama knew that Sani and I sensed something was terribly wrong. Domestic violence is very common in Asian countries, even more so than in Western countries. When a man marries a woman in India, he owns her. For some men, a woman is nothing but a toy. Women generally don't fight back. They let the men have their way.

My mama suffered physical, sexual and emotional abuse. Every weekend when Dad came home from being stationed along the border, the first thing he did was start drinking. Drinking led to verbal abuse, verbal abuse escalated to explosive, violent outbursts, and finally he beat, slapped and kicked my mama. Overwhelmed with fear, my mama made up her mind to run away like the street kids do. One weekend when Dad had gone shopping with Sani, my mother asked me to go into the kitchen and eat an orange. She instructed me not to come out of the kitchen until I was done eating. By the time I had peeled off the orange and managed to finish eating it, she was gone.

I never saw her again. I could not comprehend why. Why did she leave without taking us with her? What did we do wrong? Why this? Why that? Only questions lingered in my small head. The sudden departure of my mother left a scar in my heart that has haunted me still to this day. Then I camouflaged my heart to hide my pain and anguish. I could never let it be known what I was feeling deep inside.

Before my mama left us I do not recall the details of who was who in my extended family. At four I only knew my mother, father and my sister. However there was one man who I thought was my uncle. We used to call him Jungay Mama meaning "uncle with big mustache." Later on, we found out Mama married this "uncle."

By the next week my dad sent Sani and me to be with Aunt (name unknown) and other relatives in the mountains of Nepalgunj, Nepal. My dad's younger sister traveled to India and took us to her home in Nepal. I was to find out later in life that the original plan was to

11

take the entire family back to Nepal, including Dad. But because of Dad's work he was not able to go with us.

The trip involved almost three days of train rides and lots of walking. We stayed with her for three to four months. During our time with her, I took cattle to graze in the fields, and sometimes I would ride on the back of a water buffalo while it grazed in the field.

After several months we moved again to a remote mountain at Parbat district in Nepal near Kathmandu, where more of my dad's relatives, my grandparents and "uncle" lived. My aunt had been instructed to care for me and my sister until our father could come and get us. She was supposed to take us directly to our grandparents' place in Parbat district of Dhawalagiri Zone. Instead, we ended up at her house in Nepalgunj, Nepal.

Nepal is a country of soaring mountains, beautiful valleys and subtropical jungle. Its steep terrain, lack of natural resources and inaccessibility had meant that it had remained one of the poorest and least developed countries in the world in the 1960s.

Parbat district is one of the 75 districts of Nepal in the western mountainous area. At that time, it was the least developed districts in Nepal, about 114 km west of Kathmandu. Since the district is hilly, the land is not very fertile and it yields very little. The district is very mountainous and not very easily accessible by cars during that time. Sani and I walked up and down the rugged mountains for what seemed like days. The journey was very hard for me. I had sandals on, definitely the wrong shoes to climb the mountains of the Himalayas. My feet were sore, and I was very tired.

Sani and I were supposed to stay with my grandparents until our dad was able to come get us. However, our stay was short lived. Our relatives, barely able to feed and house themselves, were not willing to keep us. No phone calls had been made, nor had any letters been exchanged regarding our arrival. Our father had assumed his parents would care for us, but that was not the case.

Our "uncle" persuaded my eight-year-old sister not to stay there because we would not get a proper education or proper care because they were too poor. As I was reunited with my family later in life, I came to know that my aunt had her own reasons for not initially leaving us with my grandparents. My grandparents had some gold and silver saved up for us to inherit even though they were poor. In Nepal, most grandparents instead of leaving something for their own sons, save it for their grandkids simply because their own kids normally live with them unless it's a girl or daughter who marries and leaves and then the parents have to pay the dowry to the groom's family. Grandparents might have had few pieces of silver and gold and some have 100% copper cookware which is passed down to grandkids, but they do not have enough money to sustain themselves.

But once my aunt found out about the gold and silver after she brought us to them, she had a brawl with our grandparents because she wanted this inheritance for herself.

After "losing" the gold and silver, she cooked up a plan. We were a burden to her, and she felt that it was not her responsibility to take care of us. Instead of taking us back to my father, we were then taken to Nepal's capital, Kathmandu. Everywhere we went, we walked; there was no transportation. A few days' journey later, my aunt made us stay in a government shelter at Tripureshwaor alongside of the Holy Bagmati River outside Kathmandu for few days with strangers. While there, our aunt made arrangements to leave us.

MY COUNTRY: NEPAL

By Kisan Upadhaya

Imagining with my vivid mind

The paradise I once left behind

The breathtaking mountains covered with snow

Long narrow rivers where soothing water flow

Golden reflections on the snowy mountains

Glorious falls and plenty of water fountains

Different shades and multicolored wild flowers

Evergreen trees and monsoon showers

Butterflies and crickets, birds and the bees

Flying around the garden and the trees

Buffaloes and cows grazing by the fields

Terrace full of rice and corn it yields

Round and short brown pretty faces

Adults and children of all ages

Temples and stupas diverse in religion

Kathmandu, Nepal the wonder of all creation

In Tripureshwaor she arranged for Sani, only eight years old, to be ceremonially married off to a 28-year-old stranger who could not even afford to feed himself. (This ceremonial wedding meant that when my sister reached the rightful age of 11, she could then have a real wedding.) I did not understand that my sister was being forced into marriage. Once the ceremonial wedding was over our aunt left us just as my mother had done.

The first few days and even weeks in Tripureshwaor seemed normal, but as the days went by I realized I was not getting the attention and love I had gotten when I was with my parents. I was not getting enough to eat.

Tripureshwaor is located on the Bagmati River, which is considered a holy river both by Hindus and Buddhists. Alongside the river, a number of Hindu temples and shelters are located for poor people to live. The shelter where I lived with my sister was long with three walls but open at the front of the shelter. It was beside the river itself, which is also the place where Hindus are cremated on its banks.

shelter

There was one bedroom attached at the end of the building with all four walls and a door where a mother and her two sons lived. One of these sons was to be my new brother-in-law. The two brothers slept in one room as the mother slept on the floor. The elder brother was already sick with cancer and the younger brother went around with a tray of garlands, flowers and red powder from the temple. He walked house to house giving tika (red powder mixed with rice) as blessings from the gods, thus collecting a few pennies as a donation as means of work.

I lived with these two boys and their mom for short time once my sister was married to the sick older one. Thus they became my new family not by our own choice.

One day, I saw other kids having fun, jumping in the river and swimming, so I also decided to go swimming but I did not know how to swim. The river was raging high with monsoon rains that summer. I watched the other naked kids swimming in the water so I also took a leap and jumped into the river. Too late, I realized I was being caught by the current and started to yell. A passerby jumped in and rescued me from the raging water. I learned quickly not to jump in the river without knowing how to swim. It was a narrow escape.

Once again, I asked myself, "Is this my bad karma that all these bad things are happening? What have I done wrong? What is next?"

With very little clothing and little to eat, I begged to get a job at a tea stall in a nearby shop. My sister worked as a house cleaner and used what little she earned to take care of me. The sweet shop sold various different types of sweets, coffee, etc. I was a dishwasher and bus boy, a servant boy. I earned 16 rupees a month at my job, which amounted to less than 20 cents in U.S. dollars. I was very content to at least have free food and a shelter.

The job was not easy for me as I was just a child. I had never washed dishes and served customers before. It was cold and I had neither shoes nor warm clothes. I did not realize that there were consequences for minor accidents while working for others. I worked in this tea stall for a year.

Tea stall

This is the exact location in Tripureshwaor, Kathmandu where I worked as a laborer.

I left the shelter by the river and now lived and worked in the tea stall. Guests beat me up for minor accidents as I spilled tea or coffee while serving. If I broke a glass while washing the dishes, I would be yelled at, kicked and slapped by the owner of the shop. I had now become one of the street children, a vagabond without a destination.

Sometimes when I broke a cup by accident, I would not even be paid in order to pay for my damage. In Nepal water tanks are mounted on roof tops. They are made of tin and the water gets very cold in the winter. There was no hot water to wash dishes. My feet and hands hurt just touching the cold water during wintertime. I was barefoot and my feet would get wet and cold. I slept on a hard marble table at night with little to cover me except a potato sack from the bitter winter cold.

In Kathmandu the months between November to February range between mid 20s to sub 0°C temperature. The work hours were long. I battled constantly to do my best so that I would not be beaten up, slapped and lose my little salary. As a result of the conditions, I could not think or do my job well. I did not realize that my body and my health were slowly deteriorating. I was slowly becoming weaker each day. My hands and feet had frostbite from the bitter cold dishwater. I got very sick. My feet and hands grew rough, dry and cracked. The moment I touched cold water or any liquid, it hurt like a thousand knives. Unable to perform my daily tasks and chores at the tea stall, I knew my days of free food and shelter with its closed doors were ending.

Let me explain: the stall was a regular building with shutters in the front where at night and after hours it was closed. These shutters provided much better shelter and protection from the outside elements. The tea/coffee stall not only served tea and coffee but also sold sweets of various types. My daily diet consisted of drinking tea three times a day and eating sweets for main meal. Just the thought of not being able to secure food if I was not able to perform my duties alone was mentally challenging to me at that time. I knew deep inside myself that as I became more sick and weak, I would not be able to continue to work and secure the shelter from the cold and the free meals I was getting each day. I was beginning to wonder what might happen if I should get fired and not be allowed to work. I was afraid of going back to the shelter beside the river with its open front with no doors to keep me warm at night and no food to eat. I was not prepared as a child for what tomorrow held for me. Thus it was very emotionally and mentally challenging for me. How would I survive tomorrow and days to come? Although I was not treated well at the place of my work, I was fed and had a shelter to sleep.

I knew if I didn't push harder and harder, I could not continue to work. I needed to forget the pain. I felt this tremendous stress as a child. I have since learned as an adult now that childhood stress is no different than adult stress. The sun that had shown so brightly for me with a little job and some security was slowly hiding behind the clouds and the jagged peaks of the mountains that were thick with winter snow overlooking the city. As a street child trying to shelter myself from the bitter cold, the lights were slowly dimming and the glorious days of being able to get two solid meals a day were fading.

I was not feeling well. I felt cold all the time and shivered at times. I was sick with pneumonia and my body swelled up like an elephant. I tried hard to continue to work so that I could get free food to eat while the guests bullied me and made fun of me but I could not. I was fired and left to fend for myself all over again.

I became a street kid just like the others wondering around and resorted to begging for my meals. No mercy was bestowed on me by the wealthy. I went from being a self-imposed child laborer to a street child. The temple was a good place to find something to eat occasionally if you could get there before the monkeys got the food. Religious people normally came to the temple in the early morning with fruits and sweets as an offering to their gods and goddesses. Once the devotees make their offering, they would leave the temple and street kids would run inside and take whatever they can scavenge. I remember going to such a place looking for food many times as a kid. Stealing from gods and goddesses was not the right thing to do but I had no choice in order to keep alive.

My sister on the other hand continued to live with her so-called husband. She got very little to eat or money to support herself. She worked as a maid for various people just to survive and take care of me. Neither my sister nor I knew what her "husband" did for living before he got sick. I remember my sister's husband, his mom and the younger brother going to some military place not too far away and they would both bring back full plates of rice and beans that the government provided once a day.

With nothing to eat, starved, hungry and too sick to work, I resorted to begging for food on the streets in Kathmandu, Nepal. I became one of the scavengers like many other kids on the streets, hovering around every nook and corner of the street. My greatest desire as a child was to secure a palm full of rice and find shelter from the weather and the terrible living conditions.

Child begging

I searched through garbage for food beside the street dumps along
with other barefoot kids. Old buses and trucks blew out thick exhaust
of diesel smoke creating dark fumes and smog-ridden streets.

Fires burned in all corners. The city smelled like a garbage dump everywhere you turned. I searched for bugs and insects hidden in a pile of rubble hoping to find something edible. I lay on the porch of the government-built shelter by myself with its one side wide open while my sister lived inside the shelter in a cozy little room with her husband. At least it had a roof. I did not complain. I had no blankets to cover myself from the bitter cold of the night. My sister and her husband could not afford to feed me even though she worked as a maid, flower girl and servant. I was on my own. But she never gave up.

I wanted to go begging but was too sick. Still I had to go or else starve. That was my only choice at this point because no one would hire me seeing my condition. I tried to be humble, just as I had seen other kids do with the same sad story as mine but people turned their eyes away many times. Every once in a while someone would see you and could tell you were in dire need and they would hand you a few bucks. At times I wished I would be tossed on the blazing funeral fire and then thrown into the Baghamati River, the Hindu holy river that received all of Kathmandu's cremated bodies.

There is one thing that is certain in this lifetime: eventually we all must die. But I knew that in the Hindu religion there is epic tales, sacred scriptures and Vedic guidance that describes the reason for the existence of death. I knew the many possible destinations of the soul after it leaves its earthly existence. While the ultimate goal is to transcend the need to return to life on earth, all Hindus believe they will be reborn in a future that is based primarily on their past thoughts and actions. Some believe if you killed something or someone or even lived a bad life, you would return to the earth as an animal and be treated as an animal in your next life.

I didn't recall hurting or killing anyone so I assumed that I would be reborn again into another person, perhaps a rich person with a nice loving family. I began to think that once I was dead and burned to ashes, my life would be better since my current life was not so good, therefore, God would somehow let me have a normal and wealthy life after death. All of these things were going through my little head at that time.

I often saw cremated bodies from the front of the shelter where I lay sick. I could smell the burning flesh and taste the ash. The bodies were in plain sight. The smoke and the smell gave me gruesome thoughts. I thought soon one of those bodies would be mine. Can you imagine from a child's prospective the thoughts of being burned and cremated? What did I do to deserve this? Why do I have to be so sick? Why could I not be healthy so that I could at least work for a living? I was not lazy.

Cremation

Then again, cremation cost money. Would I be cremated or just thrown in the river for the vultures to eat? I was a little afraid of dying. Yet, deep down inside me I knew that if I were meant to die I would have died long ago. Behind every set of eyes, there is story to be told. Some unfortunate ones don't live to tell their story. But I have lived to tell mine. My instinctual determination to survive is the reason I overcame all that I did. I am not ashamed of what I did, whether as a dishwasher or beggar. Even begging requires work. I wanted to work and couldn't now because I was sick with pneumonia. I did not resort to begging because I was lazy but I had no choice.

But I was dying a slow death. I had been this sick for over a month.

Malnutrition is by far the biggest contributor to child mortality in Nepal I have come to know simply because I personally witnessed it. I have seen with my own eyes little children just like I was being cremated along with adults who have died of natural causes. Death is not an easy feeling when you know it's coming. When you can see and feel it. I lay myself down to sleep praying to the Hindu gods and goddesses to not take my life. But my prayer to dead god and goddesses was heard by the real and living God, Jesus Christ. He had a plan for me.

Hebrews 13:5 "I WILL NEVER DESERT YOU, NOR WILL I EVER FORSAKE YOU"

I did not know about this verse in the Bible nor did I know anything about the Bible and God at that time. But later in life I came to know this verse of the Bible and truly believe God spared me and had a special purpose for my life.

Jeremiah 29:11 "'For I know the plans I have for you,' declares the LORD, 'plans to prosper you and not to harm you, plans to give you hope and a future.'"

BROKEN HEART

By Kisan Upadhaya

All alone with a broken heart,

Memories which don't want to depart.

Wounded and shattered in thousand pieces,

Emotions running faster than avalanches.

Yesterday everything was in control,

Today the memories hunt my soul.

Don't quite know what went so wrong,

Focused I try to stay strong.

The love and feelings you had for me,

Why did you drop it so abruptly?

Our mutual feelings seem strong to ignore,

Despite all pledges, can't get back anymore.

Our love for each other has gone in vain

Far away never to return again

Silence fall with mournful pain

Love hurts when you can't sustain.

I was weak, starving, restless, full of pain, and my body was swollen. I wished I could crawl to the nearby dump to find something to eat. My sister and her mother-in-law did not have any money to feed me or take me to the hospital. I lay helplessly curled up beside my sister inside the cozy walls of her shelter room. I remember one day seeing a nice man who was dressed very well. I went to him, and told him that I was starving and had not eaten for days. I asked him if I could get some money to eat something. He hesitated but gave me one rupee. I bought some dried and fried chick peas and ate that as my first meal in many days.

Shivering from the cold I longed to be outside in the sunlight where I could feel the sunlight on my weakened body. At night I wrapped myself the best I could with rice and potato sacks, but it was never enough. In the day I moved toward the sunlight to keep warm. My sister would yell at me for sleeping on top of the wall with a three foot drop as she was afraid that I might fall and cause further injury to myself. I was motionless at times and did not move for hours by my sister's side. I don't remember this but my sister tells me now that I told her I loved her and she said bye to me many times knowing that any moment could be my last. My sister feared for my life not knowing what to do and how to seek help. At times, she thought I was dead because of my motionlessness. She would occasionally poke me to make sure I would move and was still alive. Can you imagine an eight-year-old girl and what was going through her little head? I was her only family. No mother, father or aunt and or uncle. Just her brother she loved dearly. Once I moved, she would find such a sense of relief that I was still alive. If I were to die she would be completely alone in a situation that she did not understand, a "husband" at the age of eight. While this phenomena continued for some time the fact that I was still sick and getting weaker and weaker caused her to lose her focus on her daily chores. Days passed. I moved and she smiled.

Temporarily relieved from her chronic stress, she could focus again on her daily chores and duties until she saw me again. She tried to feed me mixed rice and lentil beans to keep me going but because I couldn't taste the food from being so sick, I didn't want to eat it. I told her that I did not want to eat unless I had some meat with it. She went to a total stranger, begged, and told people that her brother was dying if he did not eat. "Please, sir, can I have some money so that I can buy some food for my brother?" One person gave her three rupees so she could run by a hotel to purchase some meat, mix it up with rice and beans, and make me eat it. I ate all of what my sister could give me and slept.

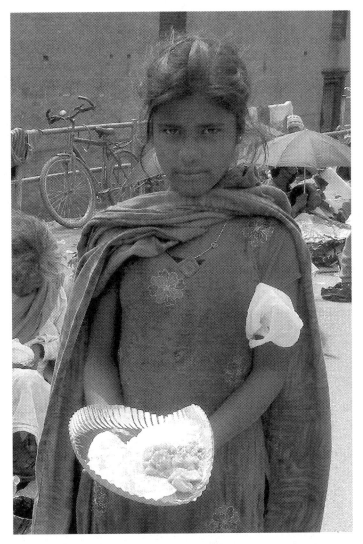

Girl begging

Meat with the bones intact is mostly served in Asia. Today my sister reminds me that I would suck the marrow out of the bone until it was white. I would go four to five days without food at a time. She reminds me now that I was so sick and hungry yet even when she brought food for me I would not eat it because I did not have the appetite to eat. At times she would have to force me to eat and would scold me to eat. While I may be mother and fatherless child, my sister played the mother's role and took care of me. Bless her heart she never gave up taking care of me.

Days would go by again and my sister would run to anyone who looked like they were dressed up nicely hoping they would have money to spare and beg again with the same story of her brother dying and not eating for days. Sometime she would go to the hotel, ask for food that was being tossed out by guests, and tell them that her brother had not eaten for days and would bring me back the wasted food by the fortunate people in order to feed me. The building still remains even today.

Finally, enough was enough and my sister and her mother-in-law decided to seek some help. They devised a plan and came up with an idea. I was coached very well. I was to tell a lie in the hospital saying that I had no family of my own. My sister's mother-in-law carried me to the hospital and told the doctors that I was found lying sick on the side of the street. She said that she felt sorry for me and brought me to the hospital as a gesture to do something nice for a stranger.

The doctors asked me if it was true or not, and I nodded my head saying "yes" that I did not have any family and did not know where they were. Lying was not something I wanted to do. But I figured it was a good lie to get help. Tell a lie, get help and survive or be honest and die? What would you choose? In any case it worked. I was admitted to the hospital. The hospital, Patan Hospital, had many doctors from overseas, many of them retired doctors working as volunteers. My sister was happy to see that I would get a nice warm place to sleep and hoped that I would soon get well. During my stay in the hospital, my sister came to visit me a few times. I noticed other kids' parents would also come to visit their children. Their visit was different though. Other kids' parents brought fruits, goodies and real food. My sister just came to visit me. I don't regret that she did not bring me food or goodies for I know she had to escape her labor and sneak a quick visit. She did not have any money to fend for herself let alone bring me something. I was content with the fact she loved me enough to come visit. She was not permitted to leave the master's house and had little relief from her servant's job. Besides, I was so sick I did not care to eat anything in the beginning even at the hospital. Like I said before I was suffering from pneumonia for over a month.

Just days earlier before I got too sick, I was looking in the dumps for food to survive and now I was in the hospital where I was given all kinds of food, which I did not want to eat. Perhaps the reason why I did not want to eat was that the hospital food did not have any spice or any salt. I did not want to eat their bland food. Heavy medications and fluids slowly got me going and my appetite returned. The doctors and nurses tried their best to make me eat. They made my eating time more enjoyable and as comical as possible so that I would eat. They knew that I was fighting for life and the only way I could survive was to start eating. Slowly, the nutritious food brought me back to life. As days went by, I became a good eater. I was once given six pieces of bread and one cup of milk, which I finished in less than two minutes. As my appetite got better, the hospital found it harder and harder to feed me. One afternoon I was given a gigantic plateful of rice, beans and some vegetables, which would have fed a family of eight. The nurses were so shocked that five of them surrounded my bed as I began to eat. They all watched me as I finished my food and looked around for some more. Slowly, I got stronger and started to run around.

All of the missionary doctors loved me and they would put me on their cart as they went to check on the other patients. I must have been one of the favorite kids at the hospital at that time because no matter which doctor went around visiting the other patients, he would put me on his cart and take me room to room while he did his rounds.

I met one patient who I became friends with who was from an orphanage. He was there as a patient as well. His name was Krishna. Later I met another girl from the orphanage who was a patient but I did know her very well. Her name was Sony. I did not know that Krishna was from Mendies Haven Children's home at that time. I just knew him because my bed was right next to his at the hospital. So lucky me. Lots of people used to come visit him with candy, fruits and other good things. Krishna's visitors also shared stuff with me since I was just there staring at them. Krishna had a very bad heart condition. I did not know what it was exactly but he was very sick. He was in and out of the hospital all the time. I met many people from his home as they came to visit me and came to know them all well.

While I was at the hospital getting better and better each day by the Grace of God whom I had not known yet, I also witnessed many young kids my age simply did not make it and died in the very same hospital room where I stayed.

ORPHAN
By Kisan Upadhaya

An orphan is nobody's child,

For he or she sees no daddy's smile.

An orphan is always left disowned,

For he or she is always bemoaned.

An orphan hangs around the streets,

For he or she has nothing to eat.

An orphan runs around on bare feet,

For no one listens to their heart beat.

An orphan has no one to call his or her own,

For he or she is all alone.

An orphan is the result of one's exile,

For he or she has no domicile.

An orphan has never seen affection,

For they are the result of someone's dejection.

An orphan is left torn apart,

For being so lonely shatters their heart.

I saw these kids die and did not know they were dead. I used to go by their bedside and talk to them as if they were still alive until someone would make me leave. They would proceed to tell me that the person on the bed was no longer living but to me they simply seemed like they were sleep as usual. I remember at least three deaths during my stay at that hospital.

There was woman from Canada (Dorothy) who also was a social worker at the hospital who really liked me and would occasionally take me out of the hospital to her home and feed me and show me around her neighborhood. Another Nepalese woman who was a discharge nurse (we called her guru ama) teacher mom, also lived in the hospital compound. She liked me and was my teacher and guardian as well. She had a young son my age named Samuel Sodemba.

We used to play together and later we became good friends as we grew up and went to the same school. The hospital was my home and I did not know that I would have to leave some day. My sister could not discharge me out of the hospital without paying all the bills.

My sister came to visit me a few more times after I began to get well but she never told anyone that she was related to me because of the fear that the hospital staff would make her pay the dues. I stayed in the hospital a long time and no one came forward to claim me. The doctors started making phone calls and found a Christian home nearby called Mendies Haven Children's Home. Immediately after the call, Mr. Mendies from Mendies Haven Children's Home and one elder girl named Dorka came to get me from the hospital.

My new life was about to begin. I had no chance to tell my sister that I was leaving the hospital nor did I get a chance to go visit my sister prior to departing for my new destination. After I began my new journey, my sister once again made a trip to the hospital to visit me. She was told that I was no longer there. She asked where I was but the hospital staff said they were not at the liberty to tell her where I had been taken. She cried and cried while walking the two miles back to where she worked. She was very emotional. Her work deteriorated and she lost her will to go on. She finally was able to tell someone that she had lost her brother. I did not know she would ever find me again and I was in a similar state of distress. But if there is a will there is a way. Luckily someone in the area knew of or heard of Mendies Haven Children's Home and told her to check there. A little over age of 8, Sani crossed the long bridge and narrow streets and finally arrived to the Children's Home, a haven for fatherless and motherless children.

You can find more information about Mendies Haven Children's Home at http://www.mendieshaven.org. Many kids who are abandoned and orphaned are brought here and given food, clothing, shelter and an education.

CHAPTER 2
How did the first Christian Children's home start in Nepal, the only Hindu nation in the world?

At a time when India was tearing apart, neighbor turning against neighbor, Hindus against Muslims and the two against the Sikhs, while the subcontinent witnessed the largest migration ever, a thirty-year-old Canadian named Elizabeth Macdonald was entering the country. Elizabeth Macdonald was working with the Salvation Army and was stationed in Calcutta, India at the time. Who came to India as a missionary just when they were trying to burn down the churches? Elizabeth Mendies, or Mother Teresa of Nepal to hundreds of kids, is known to everyone today as Mummy Mendies. She was witness to the most horrifying religious killings and the most chaotic time in India. It was 1947.

While living in the newly independent India, Elizabeth met a businessman named Thomas Mendies and in 1954, the two decided to get married. Thomas Charles Mendies was born in Rangoon, Burma and later resettled in Calcutta, India. The wedding took place on the 25th of February and on the 26th, they boarded a plane from Patna, arriving at the Gauchar Airport in Kathmandu (now known as Kathmandu Airport) about an hour later. Mummy remembers the airport terminal as a bamboo hut, which housed the immigration office. Another hut built in similar fashion served as the Indian Airlines office and every time the DC-10 flew by, it almost blew them away. Thomas was bringing his newly wedded wife to Kathmandu as he had earlier started a hotel in Lazimpat. Known as the Snow View Hotel, it was the first to cater to foreigners.

Wedded life was very difficult for both "Tom and Betty" as they became known. Tom has already opened his heart to youngsters begging on the streets of his hotel. Now he opened his heart and life further, not only in the role of a father, but now as husband. Betty's life also took on changes. In one day she not only became a routine wife but also a mother. Betty's roll of Salvation Army life became the roll of hostess, homemaker, mother, wife but still she was a missionary. In the next few years God blessed Tom and Betty. Their family grew to 12 children. Two of their own and ten adopted. God also blessed the hotel and second hotel was opened in Phokara, Nepal. It never seemed like a burden at all in the Snow View Hotel. Betty would voice what was in both her and Tom's hearts, "What is another mouth to feed around a hotel?" And so it went.

Asked what she remembers from the 1950s, Mummy looks back on those early times, almost sixty years ago. "There were few cars and if a jeep drove past, you knew right away who would be behind the wheel. There were no motorcycles or cycles. There was one flight from Patna each day, so not many people were coming to Nepal."

She remembers going to the airport to meet the incoming foreigners whom she would then try to bring to the Snow View Hotel. There would be Niger Lissanevitch who was friends with the late king Tribhuvan in Nepal who was also on a similar mission representing her husband's Royal Hotel. One cannot help imagining two tall white women standing amidst Nepali officials in their national dress outside a hut at Gauchar Airport receiving tourists arriving in Nepal. Mummy continues, "The Baghmati River Bridge which allowed only one car at a time had a white line in the middle of the bridge. Whoever got there first had the right of way, while the other car backed all the way to the other side."

Mr. and Mrs. Mendies moved in the Kingdom of Nepal at the invitation of Gen. Nara Shamsher J.B Rana and opened the first hotel in Nepal. The Snow View was a pioneering hotel established soon after the kingdom was opened to foreigners. It is at this hotel that many notables, including Sir Edmond Hillary, the first foreigner to scale the heights of Mt. Everest, would stay. Thomas Mendies was a pioneer and driving force for the birth of tourism in Nepal. His activities brought him before the royalty and many influential persons. Immediately, the street children of Kathmandu began going to the back door of the hotel to beg for food. Mr. and Mrs. Mendies would take the begging kids, walk them to the hotel, and place them in their hotel room one at a time. It got to a point where they had no room for guests and the hotel rooms were filled with kids with various needs. Elizabeth and Tom began adopting these street children until finally the government forbade them to adopt any more of the children, but the government (eventually) agreed to allow them to begin building a home for the street children.

The Mendies Haven Children's Home was born after a prayer meeting in their family room in 1967. They already had 12 kids including two of their own. After the meeting ended and everyone left, Betty discovered a little boy lay fast asleep on the living room floor. "Who was he?" "Where did he come from?" "Why was he left?" All these questions and many more came to her mind but also did the words of the commitment she had made to God every day; "Lord whomever you send we will not turn away." Tom and Betty adopted this little boy, named Amar, and that night was the start of miraculous inflow of the little lives who needed a home and love. Each came under different circumstances and through different means. Each child shared one specific common fact. They were now in the family of God who wanted them there and sent them there. I am extremely proud and lucky to be a recipient of the Mendies Haven Children's Home's kindness and generosity three years after the Home was founded.

Although it sounds like an orphanage when we talk about Mendies Haven Children's Home, it is not; it is actually a home for orphaned or abandoned kids. It is a home, founded and run on the principles and precepts of Jesus Christ. Mummy raised these children as her own. After the passing of Mummy Mendies in 2009, her grandson David Mendies along with his wife Jessica are still running the home. Mendies home does not go looking for children but through word of mouth, the kids are brought there. They prefer kids under six who are either orphaned or abandoned by families. Children are normally kept there until they finish high school. Some do stay on while pursuing further education. Once they finish school kids normally find jobs, pursue further studies on their own and get married.

Mummy called it Mendies Haven and it kept growing, accommodating more and more destitute children. She had a vision that God would send her children who needed to be looked after and she lived on faith. Initially the children's home was located in front of St. Xavier's School in Jawalakhel.

She remembered the first group of three children whom she brought to the home. Their father was a cook at the German Ambassador's residence. His wife left him and he in turn ruined his health with alcohol. With no other option left to them, the children decided to fend for themselves and walked up to the Patan Durbar Square. Coincidentally, they met their mother there, who told them to sit tight and wait for her return. It was the cold month of February and they sat outside and waited for three days. Their mother never returned. Eventually the police took them over to the police station and not knowing what to do with them, the well-intentioned officers sent them to Mendies Haven. The children were destined for a better life as the police made the right decision. With the care and education that they received, one is now in Australia, one in England and the third works in Nepal.

Mendies Haven Children's Home was initially situated in Kupendole when I entered the place. Since then it has moved to two other locations. Thirteen years ago, Mummy moved her children's home to Dhapakhel where it remains to this day.

The latest Mendies Haven comprises of three large buildings kept immaculately clean. The rooms are airy and superbly lit by natural daylight. The building near the gate houses the boys while the girls live in the other two. In one of these buildings, Mummy lived with her helpers. The dormitory is spick and span with each bed sporting a teddy bear lying on top of the pink bed sheet.

Group Mendies pic

Mummy lucidly recalled children who came here in distress, grew up, got their education, married and moved on. Most importantly, here they got love. She talks of Arjun who was born in a small village in Trishuli. He lost both his parents when he was only four. He then went to live with his uncle who did not treat him well, until one day he had the courage to run away. Dressed in rags, he slept where he could and ate what he could find. He was lucky to be found by an Australian doctor who contacted Mummy, knowing that she cared for abandoned children. The good doctor brought the kid to her saying he was very aloof. However, when Arjun met Mummy, he was immediately accepting and became attached, which made her remark, "All he needs is love." The kid grew up and won a scholarship to become an auto mechanic in California. "He came back to Nepal, became a father of three sons and is now working with a youth program here," informed Mummy with a deep sense of satisfaction. Many of the children reside in Germany, England, the U.S. and Canada. One cannot help wonder what those children would have been doing today, had they not come to Mendies Haven.

Over the years, Mummy has lost count how many children have come to stay, grown up and moved on. "But they always come back to visit. The home has big reunions on Mummy's birthday, Mother's Day and Christmas. Sometimes there are a hundred, sometimes a hundred and twenty-five. You never know how many are coming home to visit," said Mummy.

They were a loving and caring couple with the heart and desire to help needy children like me who was on the streets begging, hungry, and starving in the kingdom of a remote third world country called Nepal.

In 1981, Mummy's husband, Tom passed away and Charles, her son along with his wife Susan helped her run Mendies Haven. Mummy Mendies died in 2009 and I received the call at midnight when she passed away. I was on my way to Nepal the next day to pay my tribute to my mother who cared for me when I had no hope and no chance in life. She was and became the mother I never had since I was separated from my biological mother.

After Mummy Mendies passed away her grandson David, who is now married to Jessica now runs the home to help more children break out of poverty in the twenty-first century.

CHAPTER 3
My time in the Mendies Haven

In Mendies Haven, I found a refuge. I entered the home on December 28. I did not know my own birth date or the year I was born. They used the day I arrived at the home, December 28th for my birthday and they guessed my age to be six. They based my age on my height and my physical look and declared that I was born on December 28.

My life with many new brothers and sisters began at the mercy of Tom and Mummy Mendies at Mendies Haven Children's Home. I have celebrated my birthday on December 28th, although since I have been reunited with my biological mother and older sister I have learned my real birth date. My first week at the home, I did not know what to expect there, because there were 12 other kids there already and I was the new kid on the block.

The day after I arrived at the children's home, strange faces appeared in front of me. I could not grasp their intentions. I did not know if they meant me harm or good. I had never been more curious in my life. The house was so big and the people seemed like a crowd rather than a family. Everything seemed strange, but as time passed those faces became familiar to me. I soon found myself with dozens of new brothers and sisters. I came to learn all the rules and regulations and soon was enlisted in the group of the "smarts"—kids who are thirsting for learning. Thus, a brand new life opened for me with Mr. and Mrs. Mendies.

From them I learned about Christianity. I was no longer a vagabond wondering the streets of Kathmandu. My school career had begun. As I got older and older and learned about Christ and started reading my Bible and attending church, I came to know Christ as my personal savior. I believed in the Christian faith and learned what it is like to be saved and have everlasting salvation through the blood of Christ. Christ died for me and my sins so I would be spared. John 3:16. Once I took that leap of faith in Christ and accepted him as my personal savor, there was no going back.

As I came to know the kids, I soon recognized one kid, Krishna, whom I had met in the hospital. I also recognized a young girl, Sony from the hospital.

By the time I left the home years later, there were about 50 of us. Some were crippled, some deaf and blind, while others were either fatherless or motherless. Most of the children had relatives who would come to visit every weekend with goodies, but for children like me, there were neither visitors nor goodies. Some parents would bring fruits like apples or oranges and give them to their children while I stared at them hoping someday my mom or my sister would come to visit me and I could be like them. I have always longed to see my family since the day we were separated and I knew that someday I would find them again.

My wish came true one day when I was playing with the other kids and Purnam, a crippled boy noticed a young girl at the gate of the Children's Home and motioned me to her. My sister had come for the first time to visit me! No fruits or gifts but her presence was enough. She and I talked for a while and had a nice visit. She left again and for several weeks I did not see her. I began to wonder if she left without saying goodbye to me. Then, surprise! She showed up again. On her third visit she said she had enough of her so-called marriage and had begged her mother-in-law to take her back to our aunt who had left us in Kathmandu in the first place. Her mother-in-law agreed. She came to beg me to go with her. "Kisan, let's go home," she said. "I want to be with Mom and Dad."

However, I did not see any reason to go to my aunt's house at all. My sister was going right back to our aunt who had left us in the streets and had ran away from us in first place. The woman in charge of the Children's Home saw what was happening and came to me and asked me if I really wanted to leave.

If I left I would have nothing. If I stayed I would be fed, clothed while earning an education. At first I said yes to my sister and she went to see the woman and told her that I had agreed to leave. But later, when I had thought about things, I changed my mind and told my sister I would stay put. I thought about my time on the streets without food, when I was cold, sick and begging and I just could not go with her.

Saying goodbye to Sani was not easy. It was hard to see my sister leave me again. I did not know if she would make it home or not. I stared into my sister's eyes and said goodbye and with tears

47

running down her cheeks, she left. I did not see her again for a very long time. At least she knew exactly where I was and perhaps if she made it home, she could get my dad to come and pick me up. But that did not happen.

First my mother left me, then my aunt and now my sister. In spite of all the care at Mendies Haven, I felt very alone.

It is not what I wanted to happen, but God had other plans for me. I did not understand it then but now as an adult I do. I had many brothers and sisters to play with and talk to, yet the feelings were not the same. There was always a distance between us. I could never accept them as my real brothers and sisters. There are no feelings like sharing and loving your own family. I loved every kid at the children's home, but loving them was not the same as loving my own sister. But God gave me more brothers and sisters than I could ever imagine. And not just brothers and sisters, but a godly home where I began to learn about the Gospel of Jesus Christ and what He did for me on the cross. We had devotions in the morning and at night. No one taught me directly about Christianity; I learned just from daily prayers, Saturday morning church service and Bible reading. All of us would attend church service every Saturday because in Nepal, a Hindu country, the government is open for business and schools are in session on Sunday. School was let out a half day early on Friday and all day on Saturday. By attending Saturday's church class and the Nepalese service I began to understand Christianity. Later when I was 13 or so, I accepted Christ as my personal savior and was baptized.

Christmas was special at Mendies Haven Children's Home. Being a Christian home, we celebrated Christmas every year. The Christmas that I know now in the U.S. is not what Christmas was like growing up in Nepal. Every year during Christmas, instead of Santa coming riding on a sleigh, Santa would come riding on a real live elephant. Santa was dressed in his usual Santa suit, stuffed with a pillow to make his belly big and fat. The elephant would be rented from the zoo, which was nearby Mendies Haven and Santa would ride through the streets. It was quite a scene for the neighborhood kids to see Santa coming. Santa then handed out goodie bags for all the kids. The goodie bags mostly contained personal items like soap and toothbrushes and things that kids needed for school like pencils, erasers and notebooks. After we had sung Christmas carols and all the gifts were handed to all the Mendies Haven kids, the remaining bags would be passed along to onlookers or kids from the village who had climbed the fence wall to watch what was happening inside the compound of the Christian home. Then there would be a large Christmas feast. Friends and family of the home and kids who had gone and married would come to join the celebration. It was a truly wonderful time.

Boys and girls had their own dorms and bedrooms. Adult boys and girls occupied their own special dorm while the little boys and girls lived in their own dorms. The kids' rooms had at least one maid that slept in the same room to look after them. Girls were not allowed to hang around the boys' dorm and boys were not allowed at the girls' dorm. As the children grew older and finished their schooling, they would either get married or move out on their own. All the kids were loved and cared for very well at Mendies Haven. All were sent to the best school in town.

CHAPTER 4
The Lessons of Growing Up

I started my pre-K the same week I arrived at Mendies Haven and later went to an English-speaking kindergarten. I met a friend who would be my best friend forever from pre-K to high school. His name is Diwakar Prasai. After kindergarten, I went to the best private school in the entire country and graduated from that high school. I attended Adarsha Vidya Mandir (AVM) school which was a well known school in the country for its education as well as for its English as a Second Language studies. Only the rich kids could attend that school during my time.

Yet, I was one of the privileged kids who also got to attend it as well. Once in 2nd grade, I was promoted to the 4th grade but I told the teacher and the principal that I would not move without my best friend, Diwakar. So, they promoted him to the 4th grade as well! School life was fantastic for me. I found many new friends to chat and hang out with.

At times, there were challenges in school.

Once when I was in 7th grade, the class captain, Deepak Silwal tried to bully us. He was very big, tall and older than the other classmates. We were often beaten up and teased by him. Part of the reason I also got in trouble with him was the fact that he towered over us and was older than all of us in the classroom. He had a beard and mustache which we all did not. I along with other little ones would laugh at him for his mature age because he should have been in 12th instead of 7th grade. He was aware of it and most likely felt ashamed at the same time. But instead of learning to deal with the fact of his age, his way of showing his maturity was to bully the little kids instead. Another contributing factor in his bad attitude was that he was in boarding school meaning he lived in school with other kids while we all went home after school. He owned the school so to speak. His little followers, trying to be on his good side would constantly remind him that he was the man no one can get past in school.

He also had help from his other boarding schoolmates to encourage him to bully others who were not in boarding school as well. So one day I asked my brother from Mendies Haven Children's Home to come and settle things with this bully. My brother, Gokul Ghale was very short yet he was very strong and a great fighter from the Ghale tribe in Nepal. They are considered to be very strong and not scared of anyone. In those days only a few tribes with last names like Ghale, Gurung, Thapa Magar, etc. were hired to serve in the military forces because of their bravery and fearlessness. When Gokul was just a teenager his own biological brother got beat up by a much larger guy in town. When Gokul found out about the incident, little as he is, Gokul went looking for that person in the town and chased him out of town and broke his arms for beating on his elder brother.

At this time in my story Gokul and I had become friends and he had just started hang out with the kids at the Mendies Home off and on just because of our friendship. He was not part of the Children's Home at the time but later ended up staying there even though he had his entire family living around the corner from our Home. I asked him for a favor and he came to my school to talk to this bully and asked him to leave me alone or else.

Initially Gokul simply talked to the bully and advised him to leave me alone or there would be serious consequences. Side by side the bully and Gokul looked like David and Goliath. After Gokul had left the school property and was on his way home along with me and another good friend of mine, I heard the roar of several boarding school kids along with the bully who came running outside the school property. Some of the little followers at school had convinced the bully that he was much larger and could take on my short fighter friend. Bully was ready to fight after all and get things settled. It was a nice and satisfying street fight to watch and see the bully get beat by my brother right in front of all his classmates. After a lot of punches, upper cuts and kicks, Gokul broke his nose.

Deepak the Bully was bleeding badly as he ran to the school principal and told him what I had done. The principal did not like it and I was called into the principal's office. I was slapped so hard by the principal my ear bled. This was the hard part of being in the best school in the country. I had violated all the school rules by getting another student beat up and the principal was about to expel me. Was I ever in trouble!

The principal said, "Kisan, you better bring your mother, dad or your guardian to school A.S.A.P." I said, "Yes, sir."

Two days went by but I did not bring anyone at school with me.

The principal called me in again and said, "Kisan, where is your guardian that you were supposed to bring with you to school?"

"Sir, Mr. and Mrs. Mendies are out of town," I said,

The principal said, "Bring the next person in charge of the Children's Home then."

"Yes, sir."

I went home and got Gokul, the same person who had beat the mess out of the bully to dress up in a suit and tie and I coached him to be the next person in charge. Only problem was that Gokul could not speak English. The principal could only speak English. So Gokul and I went to school together, with Gokul pretending to be my next of kin.

The principal said, "Sir, do you know what Kisan has done? He will be expelled from school."

Gokul said in broken English, "No, sir, I did not know. Please give us another chance. I will make sure this never happens again. I will personally beat the mess out of him once he reaches home."

The principal said, "If this happens again, none of the kids from the Children's Home will ever attend this school. Do you understand?"

"Yes, sir and I will make sure this never happens from any of the kids from my home ever again," Gokul said.

So I was not expelled. Sigh! Whew! Relief.

Then Gokul added, "Sir, if these two are not getting along, why not put them in different classes or separate them?"

The principal said, "Good idea."

I was in the 7th grade, Section C, which was a big class with 65 students. I was moved to section A. Section A was for the best students, Section B was for the second best and Section C is for the barely making the grade students. I was promoted to Section A thanks to Deepak the Bully!

Once among the elite of the elite in the school my grades improved. I excelled and learned more and more. However, the fight continued because the bully still existed and I had made him very angry. Even though I was now no longer in the same class, his friends continued to taunt me and harass me all the time. So to solve this problem I asked another friend to come to school on my behalf, but this time I was smart enough not to let anyone know that I knew this second person. My second friend and I did not talk to anyone at school but he showed up and stirred up controversies with the other bullies who kept trying to mess with me. I laughed but my friend pretended not to know me and harassed me in front of them as well to make things look like I had nothing to do with it.

But soon they figured out that it was me that created the situation. So they went to the school across from ours and got another student to pick a fight with me. But since this did not happen on our school property, my principal did not care. My second friend beat up the other school kid and he met the same fate of the bully in my own classroom. I had my revenge again. But this time my principal did not say anything nor do anything because it did not involve his student. Finally, all the students were afraid of me because they knew the moment they messed with me, they would get beat up by someone I knew who was stronger than them. I was able to walk with pride—a hero with whom no one messes with anymore. School kept grinding on and ended with everyone graduating and everyone getting along. The bully in my class happened to meet me face to face on the wrong side of town one day. He apologized and we became best friends. Then we all had to prepare for the High School (SLC) School Leaving Certificate exam. We studied late into the night. For every 100 students who take this SLC exam, only 40% pass the exam, 60% fail. Most suffer difficulty in English or Math.

I passed it in the Second Division. Whew! I made it! If I had failed the exam, I would have had to wait another year to take it again. My friend/guardian Gokul ended up taking the same exam three times. As I was growing up in the Children's Home more and more responsibility was added to my daily tasks. Any time a kid was sick and had to be hospitalized, I would be asked to take food to them and sometimes I even had to stay over at the hospital with them. I spent many nights there. It brought back old memories of my time there so long ago and I knew most of the doctors, nurses and staff. When I stayed there overnight, I would take the blood pressure cuff from the nurses and they would let me check the pressure of the other patients. My nursing instinct and wanting to save lives and care for other sick people was something I wanted to do as a child. Perhaps that is what led me to work as a nurse later in this chapter where I am proud to say I saved a life.

I would even cook and eat dinner with the nurses and staff. My life was busy and full of activities all the time. It was great experience growing up in such a nice home.

Well, high school was now over and college began. I was told that the Children's Home would educate me until I finished my high school and then I was on my own. However, I was not prepared to be on my own yet. They realized this and gave me yet another chance. They prepared me to attend Tribhuvan University in Nepal. I attended college while still living in the Children's Home. College was quite different from high school. I was not the best kid in college this time. It seemed like I was always in trouble with the other students and teachers. Just trying to gain popularity among your friends and other students was a job in itself. Many students had girlfriends, money and fame. Most of the students knew that I was an orphan, without money and fame. But the best was yet to come for me.

Mendies Haven was equipped with two cars, a Toyota Jeep and a Toyota Corolla sports car. It also owned a motorcycle. As I was an older boy at the Home, I had the responsibility of biweekly grocery shopping for the home and I could take the car or Jeep to shop. I made a point to drive the car/Jeep to college on my way to shopping thus making myself look like I had money to my friends and the other students. It made a big impression on the female students at the college.

Even the rich kids could not drive cars to college and here I was driving more than one car and a motorbike to college. Oh, yes, the girls liked it and so did I. In Nepal at the university, we had three shifts of college for those who worked. Morning college was for those who taught or worked during the daytime. Evening classes were for those who worked by day. I came up with all kinds of excuses to take at least one class during the morning and one during the evening shift so that I could rest during the day shift. I spent most of the day, 6 am to 6 pm at college. Except for when I was running errands for Mendies Haven, I rested during the daytime.

At this time Mendies Haven used to have missionaries come to spread the word of God and go trekking and camping for months at a time in the Himalayas every spring and fall. I worked as a part-time tour guide and took tourists up and down the mountains of Nepal spreading the gospel. At the end of each journey, I got tips from the tourists in dollars. Twice a year I had some cash to party and show off with friends and girls. During my trip, I missed class for a month and when I came back to college I would borrow other student's notes. Boys never took notes but girls did. I would ask the girls to give me their notes from the lecture I missed while I was gone. Once a girl gave me her notes and in the middle of her notes she wrote me a love note. It was nice to have someone who liked me in the morning class and I started seeing her. However, during the day shift, I had my eyes on another girl but she was playing hard to get. So I sent her a note through another fellow and she slowly began to take an interest in me. I had two women who liked me.

Since I drove the Jeep or sports car to college at night, I thought I could pick up a date from the night college shift as well. And because of the cars, my luck turned out to be good. I was *it*. Three girls to date in college. All my friends were jealous I had three lady friends and they had none. I did have three great guy friends who were my best friends and we always hung around together and did things together. But men get jealous of each other when girl friends are involved. I had three girl friends and they had none. Someone told each of my girl friends that I was seeing someone else other than her. All three dumped me. I was heartbroken. So much for my burgeoning college social life.

As I previously mentioned Mendies Home used to sponsor groups of missionaries to come to Nepal and send them to different parts of the Himalayas to spread the gospel of Christ in various different groups. Being an adult and able to speak fluent English, I was among many other kids to take these missionaries to different Himalayan mountains and villages. I guided and interpreted a trekking expedition for months at a time. As a guide I would have my own team of porters to carry our books, cooking and sleeping tents and fuel. We would hike for days and camp by night. During the course of the day as we hiked with the missionaries, we would pass out the gospel booklets and share the gospel with people as we travelled throughout the Himalayas. The trips were always fun and I made many friends from overseas. I enjoyed doing what I was asked to do and did it well.

Christianity was persecuted during that time in Nepal and I remember one missionary getting locked up behind bars for proselytizing or attempting to convert people to another opinion or religion. I remember going to visit him at the Patan jail and taking food. It was during that time where Charles Mendies, the son of Mummy (Elizabeth Mendies) and Tom Mendies was also bearing the challenge of being a Christian and preaching the gospel in our one and only Hindu nation.

Many changes were taking place during my time in Nepal and I happened to see it all. Many Christian homes were destroyed during that time, but thanks to religious freedom, there is now religious tolerance in Nepal.

Along with my trekking adventures twice a year during college, I also took on a part time job as a nurse trainee. A friend of the Mendies family, Dr. Dick Marten, who was a general surgeon from the U.S. had setup a clinic in Kathmandu. I was to work for him doing odd jobs, consisting of cooking, cleaning, and grocery shopping for his family. Moreover, the doctor would have some students who came to intern with him at his clinic. I was able to learn to care for his sick patients as well. During this time when I worked for this doctor, he had a very sick patient with pulmonary tuberculosis admitted to one of the best hospitals in Nepal, the same hospital I was admitted to when I was young. It had moved to a new location and was called Patan Hospital. The staff and the doctors at the main hospital had given up hope for this individual. He was around 40 years old and had been steadily losing weight. Dr. Marten managed to bring the patient to his clinic. Dr. Marten looked straight at me and told me the medical status of this patient. He was dying and Patan Hospital had given up hope. Then he turned the patient over to me. "He is your patient from this day forward," he said. Wow pressure! Lots of pressure. He told me that I would have to give the patient shots twice a day and feed, feed and feed him. I had to weigh him twice a day and make sure he gained weight. His immune system was slowly dying and he was not able to fight back the disease because he had lost so much weight. I was to feed him well with lots of meat, protein shakes, and milk and make sure he ate every bit of it whether he liked it or not. His lungs were full of liquid and he was breathing through a pipe that was coming out of his back and going into his lungs. I had to dress and clean the puss and take care of it as well. It was a very infectious disease indeed. The patient hated to have me as his nurse since I was being trained on the fly without a proper education.

The only book I had was called *Where There Is No Doctor*, a pictorial hand book that most medical students use in Nepal during their early stage of training to be medical doctors. I had to learn how to give injections. If these are given into the muscles, it can hurt for days. So in the beginning I was not a good nurse to this patient but gradually I got better and better. The young man was gaining weight and getting healthier in front of my very own eyes. A few months later the man gained full recovery and walked up a 16,000 ft. tall mountain to be with his family. He came back to visit later with his entire family. I realize now such a miracle could not have been done by me or the doctor who was training me. It was a pure miracle from the grace of God that this patient made it though such an ordeal. For me, love overcame the hardship of caring for someone this sick and not being fully trained.

Over the course of my training I was able to take care of many sick and wounded kids from the nearby village. I spent many days travelling to various villages and mountains with this doctor who went places where there were no medical facilities and performed many surgeries. I was in charge of sanitizing the equipment in a pressure cooker. While one surgery was done we had to get the equipment ready for next one. I wanted to be a doctor but God had a different plan for me. I left that job and continued with my life in college and did whatever else was needed to be done at the Children's Home. I wore many hats those days juggling college, part-time nurse training and cooking at the Home (more on this soon). At least I was paid to do something important. I was thankful to God almighty for the privilege of saving my life many years ago so I could save others.

While college life offered me a social life and girls, the fact of the matter was that the Children's Home was suffering difficulties. Our cook had gone and there was no one to cook food for the kids and staff any longer. As a senior kid at the home, I was asked to take on the role of the cook. Remember, I had only cooked for Dr. Marten's family in an emergency. The deal was that if I cooked for 12 months, I would be on the first list to come to U.S. if someone sponsored me. With that said, I diligently accepted the role of master chef. Cooking rice on an open fire in a large cooking pot was a testing time for me. I did not know how much water to add to the rice. The rice doubled as I added water and soon it spilled over the pot. I took another pot and began to divide the rice into another pot. A few minutes later, the amount of rice had tripled and had started to overflow from the second pot. I ran and grabbed yet another pot and started dumping rice into another pot but I forgot to add water in one of the pots. What a hot mess! I knew that all the children were going to kill me for feeding them partially cooked rice, a bit like Chinese sticky rice I suppose. Half of the rice was sticky while the other half was uncooked. But as the days passed, thanks to trial and error, I became a good cook and everyone began to love my cooking.

I also did some shopping for the Children's Home and I was responsible for the food stock room. I was to decide what to cook and how much to cook. Of course, I was not alone because I was one of the seniors and I could get help from the other children whenever I asked. Being a big brother, I had an advantage over the other kids for I could ask others to do what I wanted them to do. I also used to help other children with their homework and made sure they went to bed on time. I was expected to lead the devotion every morning and evening as well as cook for all of the students.

I was a good student even though I started my schooling late. I was about six when I started kindergarten. I finished high school later than a typical student would have finished, but I did complete it successfully. I was a good kid and fulfilled my obligations as needed, thus waiting for my chance to come to the U.S. Finally, my prayers were answered.

In the midst of all of ongoing excitement of possibly leaving the country and going to U.S., I had to face yet another obstacle. The Mendies family adopted me and thus I went by Kisan Mendies as my last name through school and college. When I went to apply for my citizenship, I was rejected by the city officials in my town. Mendies families were originally from India and thus they were at that time not recognized by the government as being Nepalese citizens. Because I carried their last name, I was unable to apply for my citizenship. Without my citizenship, I had no passport. Although

Charles Mendies, the son of late Thomas Charles Mendies, tried to work with the political leaders in Kathmandu to get my citizenship, it was not successful at that time. So I resorted back to my best friend Diwakar again for assistance as to how I could get my name changed to my birth name so that I could get a citizenship in Nepal. Luckily for me, Diwakar's uncle was a mayor of the town I was living in at that time. By my best friend's request, the mayor wrote a letter confirming that I was born in that city and thus witnessed me growing up with his nephew to the chief of police in Lalitpur. With that letter, I applied for my Nepalese Citizenship and got it. Once my citizenship was granted, I was able to apply for my passport.

Charles Mendies was friends with all the U.S. Embassy staffs including the U.S. ambassador. Even after I had my student visa and sponsorship letter along with financial support documents, the ambassador gave him a hard time granting a visa to me saying that once I went to the U.S., I may not come back. I don't know the details as to the discussion that took place between my elder brother Charles Mendies and the ambassador, but I remember getting a message to get changed and to immediately arrive at the U.S. Embassy after hours when all of the staff had already gone home for the day.

It was raining. I wore my one good suit and was riding a bicycle with my passport in my pocket. Thirty minutes later I arrived at the embassy soaking wet as my brother and ambassador sat in his office. Somehow my brother managed to talk him into stamping the visa on my passport that evening.

CHAPTER 5
The U.S., A Completely Different World

Every year a team of teenagers from all over U.S. would come to Nepal for summer short-term mission work at Mendies Haven. Teen Missions International sent these teams each year to do work projects for the Haven. http://www.teenmissions.org/

Each team consisted of 30 teenagers and six adult leaders. In 1986 Teen Missions sent a team led by Dr. Frank Starmer and his wife Ellen. In 1986 the work project was to construct a driveway and courtyard, finish the plumbing on a bath house and toilet block, and dig a septic tank.

I happened to be the interpreter and translator for this team. Many of the Mendies Haven kids would become attached to the Teen Missions kids and we would dream of spending our lives together. Always when the teams left we would keep in touch for a while, but usually our relationships dwindled over time. In 1986, the mission trip ended and we took the team to the airport and said our goodbyes.

I always dreamed that one day I would go to the U.S. Little kids were adopted by Europeans and Americans all of the time from

Mendies Haven but no one was ever interested in me. I watched one after another kid go to Germany, England, the U.S. and many other places to start life with their new adopted families. I kept waiting for my turn but it seemed like it was not going to happen. Perhaps I was a bit too old for adoption. Perhaps God had already showed me his favor by sending me to the university.

But the Mendies were thinking of their cooking agreement with me and they spoke to Dr. Starmer, the team leader, about helping to educate a few of their older children who had finished their regular education. Dr. Starmer asked me if I wanted to come to U.S. and go to school. I looked at him and said, "Sir, I am an orphan and do not have the means to come to the U.S. to go to college." I wrote to Dr. Starmer and asked him if someday he would be willing to sponsor me to come to the U.S. and go to school. Nothing came up for a while and I forgot that I was destined to come to the U.S., so I continued with my life and kept attending college. But something was happening even though I did not know it.

Here is the story from Dr. Starmer himself of how I got to the U.S. (This below paragraph came directly from what Frank emailed me)

*   *   *

The entire affair was amazing. As you know, Ellen and I were the team leaders for the Teen Missions group to Nepal in 1986. When we got to Mendies Haven—we knew nothing except Charles [Mendies] wanted a road, some septic tanks and showers. Therefore, we did all he requested. I would go to the main house in the morning and work out with Charles and Susan on what to do and we did it.

Along the way we met you, Kaluram, Amar, and a couple of the others (Harka, I remember). During one of our morning conversations with Charles and Susan, I asked how we might help in the future. Charles said he would like some training for some of you guys so you could set up small shops in Kathmandu. He wanted auto mechanics.

When we got back to Chapel Hill, I went to Durham Tech and talked to the student advisor about whether we could sponsor students to go to Durham Tech (I have forgotten his name, but a nice person). He also said that because I was a resident of North Carolina and we would be sponsoring someone, we qualified for "in state" tuition which made the school affordable.

So I sent a note to Charles that we could sponsor someone and it turns out that Charles wanted us to sponsor two (I may have the details wrong but I think this was the arrangement). Charles said he would get tickets for you guys through his travel agency, we decided on when you would arrive: you came, got off in Charlotte, and you know that story.

At Durham Tech we signed you up for auto mechanics but I think the first day, you and Amar said you wanted to do microcomputer technology, so we switched you and I rather taught you at home while you were learning at school. We had a computer a home that you could use to learn with and our son Michael was also learning.

At Durham Tech—the rules changed and we were told that we could no longer get reduced tuition for you guys. I do not remember what happened but we managed to pay whatever was necessary for you guys to finish your program. There was a big misunderstanding between you and me/Ellen about the tuition and you thought somehow, we were making money from your school (don't remember the details, but I remember thinking that we were treating you as our own sons and paying all the bills (except we worked out village advocate routes for each of you so you could earn your own money also). Anyway, whatever the misunderstanding was it disappeared and you finished school and Amar finished and you both found jobs. Eventually you moved into your own places.

Raising our four kids with you and Amar was—in retrospect—a very positive experience in solving cultural problems. The stress, though, was such that we thought we would not do it again if Charles asked. He never asked us to do it again, so that was that.

Along the way we invited him to come to Chapel Hill and he did. He gave a sermon at the Bible Church and sort of checked up on you guys to make sure all was OK.

At the same time Charles began to place other kids in the U.S.—Gokul, Rajen, Harka—I think all were placed somewhere.

I was doing a project in Nepal the summer of 1987 and took a message for Amar to Shanti and that stated the preparations for her coming to the U.S. (might have been 1988 I don't clearly remember). Anyway—that is pretty much the story as I remember. Ask Ellen for her version—it will probably be more accurate :)

* * *

A life changing event was about to unfold in front of my very own eyes. In September 1987, I was sponsored to come to U.S. to go to college for two years by Dr. Frank Starmer and his wife Ellen. This was a real chance for me to have good training and develop skills for my life. I felt like trying a little harder to study and I even managed to finish my studies with good grades. I realized where I had come from, and where I was going. I had to make a strong decision about the future that God held for me. Perhaps I was being tested by God for his purposes.

On September 7, 1987 I boarded a plane for the first time on my way to the U.S., "my dream land." Of course, I was so excited that I forgot where I was supposed to get off of the plane. Being a kid from a third world country and having never flown before, makes foreign travel both fun and sad. Mrs. Starmer was so organized that she managed to get someone from the teen mission group who had come to Nepal to meet me in San Francisco, California. Russell and his mother came to visit me at the airport to make sure that I did not board the wrong plane. They put me safely on the plane to Raleigh/Durham.

But the plane to Raleigh/Durham landed in Charlotte. I was told to wait until everyone got off of the plane and then I would be getting off too. Everyone in front of me was getting off except for a handful left behind. As my turn came, I had to get out letting my seatmate out. There were so few people left on the plane that I thought it was my turn to get off, so I did. I followed all the passengers wherever they went until I arrived at the baggage claim. Half an hour later, I still found myself curiously waiting for my suitcase to come through that machine that went round and round where everyone else picked up his or her bags. I rather began to get worried because my luggage did not arrive. Finally, I ran to the TWA counter and told the man that my baggage was lost. TWA personnel asked me for my tickets. After seeing my ticket, the man shook his head and said, "Your baggage is not lost. You are the one who is lost." Boy was I ever frightened. My plane had already left! I had no clue what was going to happen next. I was already afraid. I had seen a gigantic woman greeting passengers at the exit ramp when I got off the plane. Being from Nepal, I had never seen such a big person in my entire life. And after being on the plane for about twenty-four hours, I was tired, hungry and now lost. Meanwhile the Starmers in Raleigh/Durham were watching every single passenger who came out of the plane with the hope that I would come out next, but I never came.

I did not have enough money to catch another plane and stay in a hotel. My heart was pumping twice as fast as normal when the TWA agent said, "Welcome to the USA." I was crying inside although there were no tears in my eyes. I could hardly talk to the agent who was trying to find me a hotel and a flight for the next morning. Finally, he told me to go downstairs and wait for a vehicle, which would take me to the Howard Johnson motel. I slowly and quietly walked down and waited for the van. But, before the van arrived, a taxi driver approached me and asked me if I was waiting for a ride to a hotel. I said I was waiting for a ride to the Howard Johnson Motel. "This is it," said the taxi driver. "I will take you there." Stupid as it may sound, I went with him and missed my van. We got lost in town in the middle of the night. The driver seemed to have no clue where the hotel was and drove all over. It was midnight and raining heavily with thunder and lightning. Every time the driver saw a phone, he would make a phone call. I was panicking every second and I began to wonder if I had been kidnapped. I did not realize that he was trying to get directions for the hotel.

If it was not a miracle, I do not know what it was. I surely would not have made it to the Starmers the next day. What a dreadful experience.... I laugh about it now when I think of those crazy days. I speculate that losing my way was the result of being overexcited. I thanked God for the hotel, flight and the ride to the airport because it was free. I salute TWA for their excellent service. I arrived at my designated destination the next day and I settled at my host family's house. Everything smelled so fresh and clean, like new paint.

Dr. Starmer came to pick me up at the Raleigh/Durham International airport. I heaved a sigh of relief to see him there. There were lots of hugs. The first thing he did was to take us to McDonald's for real American food. A hamburger with fries! Wow, it was great! We went to meet Ellen at the place where she worked and she welcomed me with great hugs. We went home and were settled and talked and caught up on all the events of the Haven. I met all four of the Starmer children. Although I already had my driver license from Nepal, I had to get an American license. Dr. Starmer had a pickup truck that he let me drive. The seat was too far back and I could hardly reach the pedal. The first time I tried to drive a pickup truck on American roads with speeding cars and trucks was an adventure to say the least. I had a few days of practice and then took my driver's test and passed it. Later I started to drive to college on my own.

I like gardening so I remember starting a vegetable garden at their house growing cilantro plants, cherry tomatoes, and lettuce. I remember the Starmers taking us to the beach for the first time; I had never seen an ocean. My first experience in the ocean, body surfing and getting salt water in my eyes was incredible. I learned so many lessons of American life while living with the Starmers.

As I started college at Durham Tech, there emerged a need for some spending money. Frank and Ellen got me a job delivering newspapers early in the morning for pocket money. During the weekends, I worked in other people's gardens and did yard and handyman chores to earn extra money. Rachel, their daughter would help me with my English homework and grammar while I was in college. They were all in school at that time as well. For fun, Mrs. Starmer also paid me to take a guitar lesson for a few weeks. I enjoy cooking so from time to time I would cook Nepalese food with chicken curry for all of us. While staying with the Starmers I attended Chapel Hill Bible Church where I met many new friends and families. Everyone liked me and I was very well treated by my new American friends. If there were any challenges or struggles with school or if I had any technical questions, I would ask Dr. Starmer and he would help with my questions. Dr. Starmer taught me that nothing is impossible; life's struggles or any other problems are merely challenges of life. Although all was well and good, I missed Nepal after being gone for some time.

I found a note which had been posted on a bulletin board somewhere, "Nepalese student looking for other students from Nepal. If you are from Nepal, please contact me." Later Dr. Harihar Bhattarai, of the University of North Carolina called Dr. Starmer's home. Through him I met a few other Nepalese in town. It was great to see them and be able to chat with them in my native language. One after another,

I met about four other families from Nepal. We had a great time bonding and getting together. Until this day I keep in touch with most of the families I met in 1988 and we have regular visits and dinner on occasions. Later I was able to buy a motorbike and was able to drive around without borrowing the Dr. Starmer's truck. Gas was cheap at that time. One tank of gas lasted for months with my bike.

The stay at the Starmer home was very pleasant and fun. Mrs. Starmer would plan a big trip each summer and she would take me to different places such as Disney World, Washington, D.C. and many different states. One summer we went as far as Montana and Yellow Stone National Park. I have been fortunate enough to travel through 30 of the 50 U.S. states. The Starmers' kind and generous parenting to someone they did not know will never be forgotten.

While at their house, I attended a community college in North Carolina, Durham Tech, for two years and studied digital electronics repair. I was sponsored to attend two years of college. After two years of study my sponsorship was about to end. I knew that either I would have to return back home and or find a place to stay on my own to continue my education. I had already started the electronics engineering program so I wanted to finish. I prayed and God answered my prayers.

There was a woman, Jay Chanda, who was studying for her nursing degree at the same college as I was. She was in need of help with her computer projects and homework. She was from India and we became lab partners. I would help her out as much as possible thus gaining her trust in me. She was a widow with young boys. One day

I was in the cafeteria just thinking about my living situation and finishing the program I had already started. Jay Chanda asked me if all was well. I said I needed to find a place to stay and continue my education. An idea popped into her mind. She said that her job and schooling were making caring for her children very complicated. She asked me if I would come and live with her and be a big brother to her boys. I was happy to hear this. I agreed and she started to prepare a room for me to move in. It is amazing how God has worked in my life!

A few weeks later, I said goodbye to Dr. Frank Starmer and his family. I moved out and settled into the room at Jay Chanda's, not far away. I was still living in the Chapel Hill area. In case things went terribly bad I could at least call them for help.

CHAPTER 6
Work, Marriage, a Family of My Own

At Jay Chanda's my main responsibility was to take the boys to school and bring them home again. Then I was to make sure they did their homework. While I was there, I studied for the electronics engineering degree I also started to work for a satellite distribution company in Raleigh as a service tech working and repairing satellite receivers. At that time, I did not have my own car and was driving my little motor bike 45 miles one way to work regardless of rain but it soon got too dangerous on the highway to drive a small bike among big trucks. With recommendations from my teacher at college, I got a computer service tech job at Duke University and not too long after I started another job in Raleigh, North Carolina. By now, Jay Chanda's children were old enough and were getting rides to school from their friend's parents.

Jay Chanda purchased a used car for me to run around in and take care of the boys. At one time she left to go to India for a month leaving her boys with me. They were still in one piece when she got back. Watching teenage boys and getting them to listen was not an easy task! During the evening, I worked part-time whenever I could. Once Ms. Chanda graduated with her nursing degree, she started to work at UNC Hospital part-time.

She later moved to Virginia and I had to once again find a place to stay.

I had begun my work at Duke University and was earning real money so I found an apartment and started living on my own. Soon after that, I managed to make new friends and through a friend I met while walking in the neighborhood, I met a young man named Jamie Barnett. Later Jamie and I became best friends. We hung out a lot and did things together. I spent many weekends at Jamie's house and met his parents who became close to me and treated me as if I was one of their own sons. Through Jamie I met his older brother John who became my roommate. John and I became good friends. John use to own a pizza restaurant and delivery service. He worked nights and slept in the daytime. I on the other hand, had a day job and slept at night. Finding committed drivers and workers was a tough thing for John, especially during the weekends when the restaurant was most busy. Workers and drivers would call in "sick" and were not able to drive. So he asked me if I would work for him during the weekend to earn extra cash. Being his roommate, he paid me $2 more an hour than he paid the other drivers. You get a minimum wage for delivering pizza so you depend on the tips. In addition, for every pizza you delivered up to 40 pizzas, you got $.50. If you could deliver over 40 pizzas per night then for each extra pizza delivered, you got $.75. I worked Friday and Saturday nights at his restaurant from 6 pm to 6 am for almost 2 years. I earned an average of $1200.00 a month extra. This was my entertainment money. I was single and had no debt. Therefore, I partied as if I was made out of money. I did a few things that I were not too smart and found myself saying, "Wow, that was dumb!" Had I saved my money, I could have had a nice nest egg, but by spending it on foolish things, being naive and not thinking I blew everything I had worked for.

Time passed and my roommate met a girl and was planning to get married. Meanwhile I was working for Duke University as a PC service tech. I drove a service vehicle and went all over the campus fixing PC's, Macintosh's, line and laser printers for different departments.

While I was on a service call from the university to the medical center to work on broken computers, I was asked by the IT manager of a department if I would be interested in coming to work for them on a full-time basis. I would get a raise in salary if I chose to do so. I accepted and started working at Duke Hospital in the department of anesthesiology. It was a promotion with better working conditions. My supervisor liked me a lot and I was treated very well. He could see that I worked hard and almost every other year I would get 10% salary increase. While I was just a service tech at the time, I learned my way around Microsoft software and took a few Microsoft training and networking classes and became a network admin. Once again taking on another role besides being a tech got me another raise at the department where I worked. I was given the training I needed to do my job by the supervisor. I provided support for over 500 users in that department, both for Mac's and PC's. Having worked as a tech at the Duke Computer repair center, I could also fix any printer so I also did printer services for the department and saved them many service calls and thus got more money per hour for my extra support.

During this time there was a young woman named Pam Fox who had just started to work in the same department as I did. Her boss was also named Pam. Every time I was in the hall and Pam and Pam saw me, Pam Fox's supervisor would make a comment about Kisan and Pam being single. I think Pam Fox had a crush on me the first time she saw me. I think her supervisor would help her break her computer and intentionally unplug the network cables and/or power cords so Pam could call the IT tech support person, me, to her office. Suddenly I was doing more than IT work for this department. For example, I installed keyboard trays under the desks. Pam kept calling me for silly little IT problems and I was getting irritated to tell you the truth.

Days went by and I kept getting calls from her. One day she offered me a cup of coffee as I worked on her computer. "How do you like your coffee?" she said. Most folks from Asia like their tea or coffee with both sugar and cream so I asked for both. Once the coffee arrived, I tested it but it did not have enough sugar. "How is it?" asked Pam. I said it needed more sugar. So she brought me another cup, this time with the right amount of sugar.

It began to dawn on me that I might have an admirer but I was not quite getting the hint. Later I asked her where she lived and after getting her address, I found out that she lived just two streets away from me. Things have happened to me since childhood, bad things and then life gets unexpectedly better. I was hard at work with no real life direction and now suddenly I began to think of a positive future. My roommate had a pool table at his house and I asked Pam if she knew how to play pool. Lying through her teeth, she said, "Oh yes, I know how to play pool. I'm quite good at it." I invited her to my place to shoot pool and then I found out she had never held a pool stick in her life. Interesting how love affairs can begin with such a simple thing as me holding her hands and showing her how to shoot pool! Since it was Pam's first date with me, she invited one of her best friends to come with her to visit me at my house. We had a great time talking and getting to know each other. And gradually after dating her for a while I begin to like her. Pam went home and told her mother that she was going to marry the IT person she met. She was dating another person at the same time. Pam was born in Durham, North Carolina. Her mother and father were divorced when Pam was 14 years old. Pam lived with her mom at the time I met her. I do not know what her mother thought about me. I am from Asia. Would it be OK for an American girl to marry a foreigner? One that she had just met? I was pleasantly surprised to know that my future mother-in-law did not have anything negative to say. She just asked Pam if she would get to meet me. Days passed and we saw each other more. Our love continued to grow. I proposed on a cold Christmas morning in 1993. I placed a ring on a round gold ornament and it hung on the Christmas tree just like any other ornament on the tree. My future mother in-law knew about my proposal.

Christmas morning came and we all opened gifts. When all the gift bags and boxes were opened, I told Pam there was one more present there for her but it was hanging on the tree. She looked and looked but it was just an ordinary round golden ornament like so many of the others. She finally gave up looking and I had to show her where the ornament was and ask her to open it. There it was, a full caret diamond ring. "Is this real?" "Are you serious?" "Oh! [kiss] . . ." "Will you marry me?" "Yes, I will."

We waited for almost two years and got married in 1995. We sent out invitations to about 150 people and we had a nice wedding. I invited some of my old brothers and sisters that I grew up with who now lived in U.S. to come and attend our wedding. Well I mostly asked them to come so they could cook some Nepalese food for the wedding. So we had Nepalese food along with American food to embrace our cultural differences. It turned out great. I hired a friend of mine from work to take a video. Jamie did the toast as my best man. The wedding went as planned and was perfect. We had a sit down dinner as well. All of Pam's family and our friends were present along with Dr. and Mrs. Starmer my host family and Jay Chandra as my honorary mom. Pam had her set of girlfriends and bridesmaids and I had my best friends as groomsmen. But there was to be yet another surprise. My best friend had a nice rental car at that time and he had volunteered to take us to the hotel after the wedding. However, when it came time to get to the hotel from the church parking lot, a stretched limo pulled in front of us. We were so surprised! Then, after assessing the situation my new bride asked if we could stop by her grandmother's house on the way to the hotel. With Pam was still dressed in her wedding gown we pulled into her grandmother's drive and went to say hello. What a surprise for her! She had not been able to attend the wedding because of her age and poor health.

Our honeymoon had two parts. We spent a few days in the Bahamas and then we spent a few days at Disney World. It couldn't have been better. We had jointly purchased a house before the wedding and so we came home to settle into our new lives.

CHAPTER 7
Searching For My Lost Family

I had always been searching for my lost family back in Nepal, but now the internet was making my searching dreams a true reality. The internet allowed me to keep in touch with some of my friends in Kathmandu and I thought of my family constantly. What had happened to them? Where was my sister now? In March of 1997, Pam and I went to Kathmandu, Nepal. I wanted her to know for herself where I had come from and what Nepal was like. For the most part we stayed with my best friend Diwakar in Kathmandu and his home became our home base for our future visits to Nepal. We went to the Mendies Haven Children's Home where I grew up and met Mummy Mendies, who raised me in Nepal. It felt good to be back home but there was still a void in my life and I longed to find my biological family someday. Pam and I had a great time during our visit to the Home.

Pam and I sponsored a large family reunion and we invited all the kids I had known who by this point were already settled on their own. Many of them had married and had their own families. There were almost 150 people that day at Mendies Home. It was a very remarkable experience to see all of us together after so many years to say the least. These were kids who I considered my own brothers and sisters and now I am uncle to so many kids in Nepal. It felt great when all the little ones called me uncle. Wow! Marvelous!

With bittersweet memories and feelings, we had to depart again. Back we came and went on with our normal working life as husband and wife. We went to Rose of Sharon Baptist church at that time. Church was great and friends were great as well. Every Christmas I would speak in front of the church and beg for donations for Mendies Haven and then send money to help with their Christmas expenses. God really blessed us. Later in life we moved our church membership to Liberty Baptist Church. We have been attending there for last 12 years.

Our first child was born in March 29, 1999. We named him Kevin starting with K as my name started with K as well. Kevin was a joy and bundle of happiness.

Kevin

I remember a Macarena gorilla I bought for him as a gift soon after he was born. It sang the "Macarena". Raising Kevin was fun but challenging. He had colic, which meant that he cried from 6pm-10 pm daily for almost six months non-stop. Finally, he got over it. The first thing he said was Dada and Pam was not too pleased.

Today Kevin plays the piano and some guitar, and he plays soccer at school and baseball when he can. Kevin is a smart kid who is in 8th grade but is taking 9th grade math. Kevin's other hobbies include swimming, deep-sea fishing, hanging out with friends from school and church.

Besides attending a Christian school on weekdays, he is very actively involved with the church bus ministry on Saturday. Every Saturday morning he gets up early and rides the church bus and helps to pick up kids from all over the city and then also helps with their activities as well. On Sunday he plays the piano for a group from church who go visit the elderly regularly. While most kids sit at home and play video games, Kevin spends his free time serving the Lord. Wednesday evenings he goes with his friends from school knocking on doors, asking and inviting folks who do not currently attend church.

Every opportunity he gets, he wants to volunteer and help out at church or at the Christian school. For all of his work and devotion he has received an award. As you might guess I'm a very proud father.

Meanwhile, Pam and I had been trying to have one more child but we were not able to. As we talked about it, we began to have the idea of adopting a child, a baby girl from Nepal. Pam prepared the documents and got me to sign on dotted lines and I sent them to Bal Mandir in Nepal. We went through a home inspection and home study by a social service agent to see if we met the requirements for adoption. Social service workers came to our home to investigate our living standards and to see if we had a place for an additional child. In 2005 we were somewhat low on money and did not have enough to pay a trained adoption agent so I hired my best friend,

Diwakar, in Nepal to act as my agent. He was very nice to do that for us. We waited in the U.S. to hear from him. After about six months we finally got the phone call to come to Nepal to get our daughter. Her name was Sudeshma (meaning foreign land or another world). How amazing is that! She was about to leave her birth land and come to another country just as her birth name indicated. Sudeshma has a story in itself because her biological mother was a young village girl in Kathmandu who was forced to marry a person in a remote village who claimed to have lots of money and land. Her mom at 16 with no education followed the young man and ended up marrying him. Once she reached the village where the young man was from, she discovered he was already married and had another wife as well. Wow, what a turn of an event for a newlywed. By then it was too late and she was expecting a child. The agency run by a woman who helps the girls who are involved in trafficking in Kathmandu also attends the same church as I did as kid in Kathmandu, so this young expectant mother was rescued and brought to Kathmandu from another state. She later ended up in one of my older brother and sister's homes in Kathmandu who grew up with me in the same orphanage. The baby was born but no one knew what to do with it. God in Heaven was looking after this angel for her to come to U.S. Pam and I called my older brother in Kathmandu and said that Pam and I were interested in adopting a baby girl from Nepal. We asked him if he knew of anyone who is unable to take care of their baby. My brother from the Children's Home could not believe the phone call he had just received from us because there was a baby girl with them that they had no idea what to do with! God's blessings in disguise I suppose. He told us a story how there is a baby girl at his home from a young mother who could not care for the child and sent us the baby pictures. Once Pam saw the picture of the baby, she cried and said, "Let's go get her."

Now comes the hard part. You cannot adopt a child from just anyone or anywhere. There are many children's homes you can get the babies from. So my acting adoption agent Diwakar and my big brother Arjun Mendies consulted and took the baby to Bal Mandir and told the manager of the home that this baby is for the applicant they had just received. Normally the wait time is two years for paperwork to go through. Since we already had a baby picked out and were not staying at the Bal Mandir in Kathmandu, it was matter of getting a government official to sign the document in a timely manner. Happily, we only had to wait three months. However, those three months seemed very long to me. Nonetheless, the phone call finally came and we headed to Nepal to get our daughter, leaving our five year old son with his grandma. Pam and I had never been gone anywhere without our son up until this point. Once the baby was handed over to us, Pam was ready to leave Nepal and to be with our son Kevin. For me on the other hand, I have come halfway across the world to be with my friends and the only family I knew from Mendies Haven. I wanted to stay longer and spend time with them. So Pam and I once again visited Mendies Haven and gave all the kids a nice dinner party and invited many of the old kids as well. However, we had to cut our trip short and get back home to Kevin. Since I was from Nepal and knew how everything worked, I was able to move the adoption paperwork through the system and get all the necessary signatures.

We gave our baby girl a new name after my mother who raised me at Mendies Haven: Kaitlyn Sudeshma Elizabeth Upadhaya.

Both Kaitlyn and Kevin are growing and doing well in school. Kaitlyn is a 3rd grade princess who loves fashion, watching what's cool on TV and singing.

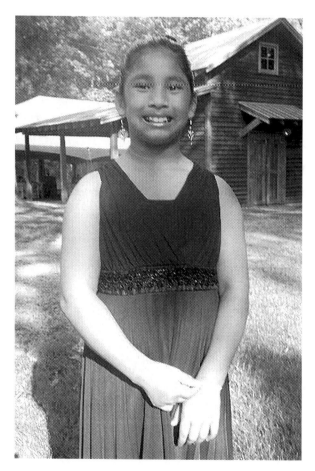

Kaitlyn

After all of the struggle in my early life, I have learned to take tomorrow as it comes. I survived and have had several lifetimes. And though it seemed like I have had enough burdens in this life, I did not think I should just be prepared for a life of ease. I believed my mission in this world was not yet over. As I reflected on my past, saw that last orange and recalled the many nights of hunger and the time that I spent out in the cold, I found myself feeling guilty about my life in "land of milk and honey," the U.S. It seemed like time passed so quickly. Not a day went by that I didn't think about the family I left behind in Nepal.

It felt like yesterday that I was naked and now I am clothed. I was starving and now I am fed. I was restless but now I am strong. Yet, the horror of the past still keeps haunting me. Should I settle down and try to forget the past? No, I did not think so. I couldn't until my biological family was found.

My quest to find my biological family continued. I continued to pray and ask God if it was His will, that I would find my biological family soon. But God did not answer. It was not the right time perhaps. I tried to go to Nepal and search myself but God did not want me to and things did not work out.

Now reflecting back on my family search that started even while I was still in Nepal at the Haven, I see that God had a plan, and a time. Sometimes when I lived at the Haven, I would go to the place by the river side where I once lived with my sister. I wondered what happened to her and would ask people if they remembered her or if they knew what might have happened to her. I was told that she went with her mother-in-law to look for the aunt that had left us on the street. The story was that my sister made it back to my aunt's house safely. But my aunt, so the story went, was not happy and paid a witch doctor to craft a magic spell on my sister's mother-in-law. Her mother-in-law had returned to Kathmandu, demon possessed and had died before I was able to talk with her.

While I was in college in Kathmandu, I began to discuss my hope of finding my family with my best friend Diwakar. We tried to come up with a strategy. In the process, we wrote a letter to the Assam police department but did not get any response. Another dead-end. After I went to the U.S. and began working with computers I began to use the internet to try to locate my family. I found a man with a name that was as similar to my dad's name that I could remember. Through the internet, I also found an address in Guwahati, Assam. I wrote a letter asking the person if he might be my dad or if was not, did he know of anyone else with similar name in that particular town working as a police officer. My letter briefly stated my separation from my family as a child and that I was looking for my dad. However, the letter was not understood by the recipient and he sent it to his grandson in Japha, Nepal. Once the grandson read the letter, he wrote me a hate letter back thinking that I was trying to claim to be a lost son of a recently retired police officer and I wanted to take a share of his pension check. So, I called Diwakar in Nepal and explained what had happened. Diwakar then searched and managed to find the grandson and explained my story to him in detail.

The grandson, Deepak Wagle, began to help me then. He put in much effort to help me find my family. In 2004 I made a special trip to meet Deepak at the border of Nepal and India to hunt for my family. However, another obstacle stood in my path. I had forgotten to check my passport for its expiration date and my passport had expired. When I boarded my first flight no one mentioned my expired passport. My passport was again checked in Chicago and again no one mentioned my expired passport. But when I arrived in Kathmandu, immigration noticed that my passport had expired and took it away from me. It takes over six weeks to get a passport in Nepal and that includes a large sum of bribes. I have only three weeks of vacation time. I did make it to Jhapa where Deepak lived after 16 hours of driving and met him personally and got to know him then. However, I was unable to cross the border since I had to return to Kathmandu and deal with immigration to get a renewed passport. I was saddened by this. God again had blocked my path. However, unsuccessful as I was on this trip, getting to meet and know Deepak proved to be the key to my successful hunt for my long lost family.

Diwakar and I lost touch. Instead I began to communicate directly with Deepak via email. Then came the Facebook era which would totally change my life. Deepak had gone to school in Assam, India, so he was familiar with the state where my parents lived. I asked him if he knew anyone in the Assam police department. He said yes, I know a relative who works there.

DEEPAK'S STORY IN HIS OWN WORDS

In fact I came to know Kisan because of the similarity in his dad's name (Indralal Upadhaya) and my grandfather's name who was also Indra Prasad Upadhaya. My granddad was also in the Assam police force in those days. So somehow Kisan found out (after a long and tiring search) that my grandfather is called Indra Prasad Upadhaya and he was in the Assam police. Then he thought this man might be his dad . . . . but he doubted it. So he kept sending my mom, my aunt and my brother a lot of letters asking them to help him find his dad. It was around the year 1999 or 2000. At that time I was working in Nepal although my family (dad . . . mom . . . . brother and sisters) were in Assam (KarbiAnglong district). Nobody paid any attention to Kisan's letter and they all thought it to be a hoax. Kisan's friend in Nepal, Diwakar Prasai, also wrote letters to my mom's sister (who lived near our house in Assam) in Nepalese language telling Kisan's sad story and Diwakar also gave his phone number to my mom, aunt and brother. Still no one bothered to phone Kisan from Assam. Then in 2002 I went to Assam during the Durga puja to celebrate the festival. My mom and aunt told me all the story about how a man called Kisan was troubling the family by thinking he was related to us, which meant my grandfather would have been a bigamist. I found out that my own brother got angry with Kisan and wrote back a nasty letter to Kisan telling him not to write such stupid things. My brother must have really written a bad letter (Kisan talks about it sadly to me even today). I have not seen that letter, though.

I asked for all the English letters written by Kisan and Nepali letters written by his Nepali friend Diwakar from my mom and after the Durga puja celebrations, I came back to Nepal. As I entered Nepal to start my teaching here, I thought of engaging Kisan to find out the reality. Then I checked the Nepali letter and found out Diwakar's phone number. I phoned him and I was told the really heartrending story of this guy called Kisan. I believed what Diwakar told me . . . so I even went to Kathmandu to meet Diwakar. Diwakar told me to bring a photo of my grandfather to see and check whether his face resembles Kisan or not (up to that time Kisan and Diwakar both thought my grandfather to be Kisan's father). Thank God . . . my grandfather did not have any secret wife and secret children. After that I talked to Kisan by phone . . . I hadn't seen Kisan face-to-face yet. I promised to dig into the matter more and find out if my grandfather really had another wife with children apart from my own good grandmother and my mom and maternal uncles. So first I waited for Kisan to come to Nepal. He came down in 2004 and met me and I was convinced this guy is seriously looking for his biological family. I was moved emotionally and did not care for the respect of my grandfather . . . who knows? He might have made a mistake secretly in his life. Then during the year 2005 we went to Assam to meet my grandfather's sister (thinking her to be the naughty aunt of Kisan) who sold the kids in Kathmandu. But surprisingly enough, I found my grandfather's sister to be too naïve to do such a smart and villainous job like the real one who did. So I returned from Assam's Lakhimpur (where my grandfather's sister lived) empty handed. But I kept the search on and still contacted some of my other relatives in the Assam police to help find a guy called Indra Lal or Indra Prasad (Kisan himself was confused about the clear name). I somehow managed time once a year and used it to go to Assam to meet my parents and always made it a point to do some inquiry about this unfortunate guy's biological family. Well, I carried on with my search because I knew how desperate Kisan was to find them. This is how I came to know Kisan.

We became good friends after that and I told him that my grandfather was not his dad. But still we liked to think of each other as relatives for quite some time. Then we lost track of each other since life got busy. I had many other things as well to attend to. Back in those times there was no internet facility at my disposal. I was out of touch with him for almost six years though a faint hope was there that my search would be successful one day. I thought it was futile to contact him unless his parents were found. During this gap of our non-communication, I moved from my remote area settlement to a more urbanized area to become the principal of a private school. Now I had more access to internet as well.

One day, I just wondered whether this guy Kisan has found his biological family or not, so I decided to search for him on the net and ask him. Luckily I found him on Facebook and sent him a friend request. He seemed to be very glad to find me on Facebook after so many years. We got to chatting and again he started making the same old request to me: he wanted to find his parents. I thought this man is strange, after so many years went by, but his belief that he would find his parents did not leave him. His conviction was again a motivating factor for me to give the job a try. This time God was really by my side when I made Assamese friends on Facebook like a crazy guy. I made friends after friends from Assam. My advantage was that I could converse in Assamese as I had my schooling in Assam in an Assamese medium school. Kisan and I had talks about posting his story on Facebook and letting the Assamese friends know about it. I made a gentleman called Pranabjyoti Goswami my Facebook friend in 2011. He is from the Assam police and was in a quite influential position.

Kisan wrote his story and sent it to me and I posted it as a note, "True Story of my Friend" on the 1st of June 2011 not knowing that this note of mine would be believed so easily by these big guys of the Assam police. But they did believe and even made Kisan their friend after I requested both Kisan and Pranabjyoti to make each other friends so that the story would seem more genuine when Kisan himself told it to the police officer. My belief was right, Pranabjyoti Goswami and another super smart Assam police guy Rajen Singh both were ready to help find Kisan's dad. The rest is known to all. Ah! I am more than glad that it could really be done with my small effort of making Assamese friends and establishing their links with Kisan.

In fact, God had his plan to make Kisan meet his sister and mom after so many years: so it was all designed in such a way that I would come in the scene and be of help. God bless Kisan and let his new found biological family and him never have any bad days! Internally, I want my children to remember me as a good dad who has been of help to someone in life.

*　　*　　*

Deepak then introduced me to a fine man by the name of Pranabjoyti Goswami, an additional superintendant of police working in the Directorate of vigilance and anti-corruption in Assam. We became Facebook friends and chatted a while and I shared my story with him. He started to dig into police records and began to get some vital information. While Parnav worked on paper trails, I was then introduced to Rajen Singh in the same police department who is also a Deputy Commandant in Assam's commando battalion. We became friends and once again, I shared my story with him as well. I provided what little info I had and told him my dad's name, my mother's name and my sister's name. I told him about some geographical landmarks as well. Now I had two people working and digging into the details. They found a few names that matched the police record. As I was being updated from India, I also got updates from Nepal from Deepak on the recent developments there.

Rajen went above the call of duty, phoned the television station owner, shared my story, pleaded with them to broadcast my story, about how I had been searching for 40 years, and had not found my family. Then God started to answer my prayers and opened the doors for me to find my family. Praise God for his love, mercy and answer to my 40-year old request to be reunited with my family.

Then on August 12, 2011, things began to open further for me. I received word from my friend Rajen Singh (through Facebook) that Newslive TV wanted to help with my search for my mom and sister. I was thrilled at the idea of someone else helping because I had tried for so many years, but when you do not know where to look, it is fruitless. I connected with Zahir Hussen of Newslive and he asked me to go live on primetime at 8:00pm and tell my story. He thought it was a compelling story and he wanted to help. For 90 minutes we went through my story and any details that I remembered from my childhood. They posted some of my teenage pictures from Facebook on the TV screen as well. They posted a phone number to call if you had any information and before the show was over, he told me they could not handle all of the calls from people calling just to wish me well in the search for my mom. One of those phone calls was a neighbor from when I was a child—they remembered me from the pictures Newslive showed. This was a huge turning point.

Another key person who saw the news was my uncle Bal Ram Sharma from Assam, India. He immediately called the TV station but kept getting busy signals. It wasn't until the next day that he was able to get through. He knew where my older sister was and the location of my mother in a remote village in Nepal. I went on live TV in India 3 additional times and eventually found my mom. From Kathmandu City it is one full day's drive to a small town in the northwest part of the Himalayas, then you have to hike the rugged mountain by foot for an additional six hours to reach her. Newslive TV sent my friend to her village to bring her to the main Kathmandu City. While she was being brought to Kathmandu, the TV station flew one of their reporters to Nepal to meet her in the hotel. In addition, my sister was located in Tinsukia District of Assam, India, a remote part of northeast India where she lives on a tea estate. We were all united via technology and Skype on that show. Because of the bandwidth and the poor quality Skype to satellite network in India I was not able to see my mom's face very well. But, it was wonderful to be able to look at them even though it is not the same as seeing them in person. When I saw them, I knew I had to go to India. My wife and I made quick preparations, got Indian visas and within two weeks, we were in India.

We arrived there in Guwahati airport at 2 pm Sept. 4, 2011 and were welcomed by Parnav the Superintendent of police at the airport followed by live media coverage of our arrival to the main town of Assam. People in Assam were all glued to their TV stations that day to see the grand reunion in person that evening. The reunion aired on Sept. 4th. I was able to share my testimony on live TV in the Hindu state of Assam in front of 27 million people of what God had done for me. He had answered my prayer. I have been able to tell all this to friends who have requested me as friends via Facebook and point them to my local church salvation message. A few have taken an interest and some have said they would go to their local church to find out more as well.

CHAPTER 8
My older sister Sani's Story

Sani means "the little one" in English. It is what I always called her and never knew her real name Maya Devi until August 19 on live TV in India when my sister first appeared on a big screen with a smile of joy and happiness. It took a lot of effort and courage to connect us. Friends and the news media were not sure if this was going to work or not in Assam, India. Maya Devi was three years older than me. Interestingly enough Maya means love in Nepalese as well as the English language. Although it has many other meanings such as divine, close to God and in Hindi, the Hindi name Maya means God's creative power. However, for me the name Maya meaning love is sufficient and she proved what her name meant at very early age towards me.

Umoti Devi gave birth to my sister in 1962 in Assam, India. She was the first-born daughter of late Indra Lal Upadhaya and Umoti Devi who was last seen in a remote village in mountains of the Himalayan country of Nepal. Maya had a loving mother and father during her childhood but something was missing in her life. A young brother she could love, play with, and cherish shared memories for days to come. She was the only child at the time until her brother was born three years later. Instant bonding for a young girl towards her brother began naturally. Life went on with mother's tender care and love both grew up happily for short time. She started school at four and walked to school barefoot just as if her younger brother did at four. Education was not part of her family life since neither her mother nor father was very educated. She managed to study up until 3rd grade in a small government school. She does not remember the name of the school or any of the teachers' names. She attended a different school then her younger brother did. After school, she played at home and in the evening time, she went for tutoring.

Maya remembers at night telling her dad to read her bedtime stories. Her dad always told her the difficulties of his young life and his own childhood and often cried a lot. He told her that he grew up very poor. He was the youngest of the three brothers and two sisters. Without much to eat, he would often go hungry as a child. My sister also said that my dad's mom (my grandmother) had died while dad was about eight years old and his dad (my grandfather) remarried. His stepmom hated all the kids including my dad. Dad and his brothers were sometimes tied up like a buffaloes are in Asia with rope and they were given grass to eat by his stepmom at times. This is the reason all three brothers left to get away from her.

Not to repeat what has been already said in Chapter One of this story, but Maya was destined to be doomed at the early age of eight not knowing what future held for her youth. She found herself rejected from her own biological family and then neglected by her own aunt, her father's younger sister. Forced into ceremonial marriage at eight and then abandoned by her selfish and ruthless aunt in Dharma shala (government-provided pilgrimage shelter) alongside the Baghmati, the holy river of Nepal where Hindus believe that Lord Shiva meditated and was born.

Sani lived with a man that was three times older and was stricken with cancer. He would die any minute or any day. Why would someone allow such a sick person to marry a young girl that had not even reached puberty? In an Asian culture in a third world country with thousands of rituals and rites, I suppose anything is possible. Even today in remote parts of Nepal such a practice of marrying their children off at young age goes on. She was not a wife but a child laborer placed in brothel so to speak at that age. No, we will never find out how much money her aunt collected from the groom's family as a dowry for selling a young child to a stranger in a strange and unfamiliar place.

I just cannot imagine what was going through her young mind. She cooked, cleaned, and became a slave. Soon her sick husband was taken to the Bir Hospital for treatment and later died. Sani found herself working as a maid doing what her in-laws asked her to do. As time permitted, she worked for various different people doing whatever chores they wanted her to do.

The life of Nepalese street children is so pathetic with the little money they made by street-based jobs such as rag picking, begging, selling flowers, etc. Even with such hard labor she could not afford even one full meal a day.

For Maya the horrible tale of her childhood does not end there.

Even the police themselves often beat, harass and even sexually assault and torture the street children. Time goes on with suffering and betrayal by her own family. No one called Mom or Dad, no one loved her or cared for her, and she had to care for herself at that age. To add salt to a wound, she finds her five-year-old younger brother is sick with pneumonia from cold and has swelled up like an elephant and there's no one to take of him either.

What can she do? Maya finally came to her wits' end and asked her mother-in-law to take her back to her parents. She often cried once her brother had recovered and was now gone to the Children's Home. She was alone. She begged her mother-in-law to take her back to Nepaljung where her aunt lived. Somehow, she ended up back at her cruel aunt's house. She was a bit excited and happy in the beginning for being closer to her blood relatives but her happiness did not last too long. Her aunt had four children of her own, three sons and a daughter. Maya was ill-treated by the aunt's children except by the older son.

While others played and went to school, Maya found herself cooking and cleaning for her aunt and cousins. She was bullied and harassed by her own family members in Nepalgunj, Nepal. At this point, she was now 10 or 11 years old. Her cousins were about 15 to 16 years old at that time. When Maya made a small mistake, her own cousins would punish her. If she dared to speak back at them or question any of her cousins, they would taunt her and pull her hair and drag her to the floors and punish her for fun.

Out of frustration of being neglected and abused by her aunt and cousins, Maya puts herself to sleep crying that night. Quietly early the next morning she ran away. She was not afraid of being on her own in order to escape their abuse and knew she had to survive above all else.

After departing the abusive home, and running away to another village, Maya was taken in by a Nepali family. She lived with them for about a year. She does not remember their names. Initially they did not really ill-treat her and she worked for them washing the dishes, clothes, tending the animals, working on the farm, and threshing the grain.

Maya washing clothes

They gave her food and clothes in return along with some money from time to time. One day while doing the dishes, she broke a cup and a plate. The family scolded her and refused to give her food that day. After she washed the dishes, she went up to the top of the house. She cried there the whole night and went off to sleep. Early in the morning when everyone was still asleep, she quietly ran away again to avoid being mistreated.

Maya worked odd jobs, in order secure a decent meal a day, and would go into the forest and collect firewood for various people carrying a load on her back. She often went to the well to fetch water for cooking without shoes on her feet.

Girl performing labor work

She washed dishes, cleaned and did laundry for people for a few rupees a day. Maya was determined to survive and make her ends meet no matter what she had to do. Hoping someday her dad or mom would come looking for her and she could live a normal life again, she thought about her brother many times when she was alone wondering what Kisan was doing these days.

Maya used the money she collected earlier to run away to Nepalgunj where she met a few people who saw her alone. When asked why she was wandering alone Maya sobbed and told her whole story. A few of those people from her village saw and recognized her and offered to help her. They told her about a family needing domestic help and pointed her to the right direction. She found the place, which was a big house, but looked like a mansion to her. She sat outside sobbing. Outside the house was a farm with a huge Bor tree. As in many other trees in India, this was rather large tree with unusually large branches. It is also used for many medicinal uses and is the national tree of India. An old woman finally came out and asked her why she was crying.

Maya repeated her story of neglect and all of the abuse she has received everywhere she went. The sympathetic old woman told her to stay with them in the house and work. Maya was well looked-after at the place and finally found the refuge she had longed for. The old woman was religious and prayed a lot to the Hindu gods and goddesses.

Once again, Maya did the dishes, and in the morning collected flowers and made garlands for the old woman's rituals. Bless her heart, Maya said the lady loved her a lot which she desperately needed it after all the ordeals of her life that she had to endure. Maya lived there for about 10 months to a year.

One day her cousins came looking for her. When they found her they asked her to come back to their aunt's place, and told her that her aunt was sick, and wanted to see her. They made it look like they really searched a lot for her and went through many difficulties trying to find her. Maya refused, as she loved being where she was at that time with the old woman. Maya told them she was fine there. However, her cousins coaxed her into leaving with them. Her cruel aunt died one month after Maya had returned to her snares.

Maya now was a bit older and getting a bit brave as well. After all what could she lose by being brave? What could her cousins do that they had not already tried on her? If cousins tried to bully her, she could fight back. She could say no if they tried to make her work too much. She demanded that the chores be divided equally with the other members of the household or else she threatened to leave.

But unfortunately Maya could not be free of her troubles.

One day she took the cow to the fields to graze to an unknown area to her; the cow strayed away into someone else's field and ate their plants and grain. Naturally, the owner of the field complained to her older cousin brother who yelled and slapped her for her carelessness. Poor kid, when was it ever going to stop? She cried and told him what was the use of living when she has to suffer by being beaten up for something beyond her control.

Maya considered suicide and felt like it was the only way out of the hell on earth she has endured already and future trauma she envisioned would come.

Maya was now an orphan, without a loving father, mother and brother. She was at a total loss and did not know what was in store for her future. I can only imagine what she might be thinking after all of her tragedies and frustrations. It would have driven me insane to even think or place myself in her shoes wondering how anyone could go through such physical, mental anguish especially at such an early age in life.

Quietly she told herself that she had lost her family, had only one brother whom she now has no contact with and had no one to look after her. With these thoughts, she went to the river near the fields and jumped into it to end her life. The flooded river swept her some distance away. She was unable to swim and was slowly drowning. But her suicide attempt failed, because some people saw her jump in and came to her rescue. The river drifted her about one kilometer away. Everyone panicked because she was asphyxiated with water, but they managed to save her. Her breathing was shallow and she was semi-conscious but still showed signs of life. The fisherman took her to the health center where the staff forced all the water out of her lungs. Later she was sent back to her aunt's house where her family scolded her again.

They said she will bring bad luck and will curse the family. When asked why she did what she did, she replied and said she did not have a reason to live. What's the use of living? Then the village people tried to make her understand that she was older now and should act more responsibly. After that, her cousins took her home and explained to her, this time more gently, the stupidity of her actions. They left her alone and did not harass her. They all divided their work equally. She lived like this for a year.

Then one day her uncle, Salik Ram, (our father's older brother) his wife Khagisara and their older son Guru from Tinsukia, Assam came looking for her at her aunt's place unexpectedly. By this time, Maya was about 15 years old. After years of talking and coaching Maya's own father to go look for her and her brother failed, her uncle decided to do something himself. Salik Ram journeyed three days by train all the way to Nepaljung, in the midwest part of Nepal. To his surprise he found Maya doing dishes as usual at her aunt's house, Salik Ram's younger sister's house. When Maya heard her name called out, she was in tears when she saw her uncle looking down at her.

He took her by her rough hands and told her that he was there to take her home. He inquired about Kisan and heard what had happened. The place where her uncle stayed is called Birgaon. She did not recognize him as she saw him only when she was very young. After her uncle explained to her and told her about himself, she remembered him. Asked about me Maya shared the story about how her brother was now in a better place at the Children's Home. Her uncle wanted to take her away and her cousins agreed. Her uncle took her back to Guwahati, Assam to her parents' place where she had lived before. Fifteen years had passed since she had left her birth place and the town had gotten bigger and more densely populated. The surrounding scenery had changed but she could remember the area.

When she arrived her father was not at home. The news of her arrival spread quickly in a small village where folks knew of the situation many years back, and everyone came outside to meet her. At her parent's house she was greeted by another woman who turned out to be her father's new wife named Man Maya. She was a bit hearing impaired but could speak. Man Maya gave birth to three kids. There were two boys Ramu and Raju and an eldest girl, Pabitra. Upon Maya's arrival at Dad's house she noticed that Pabitra her stepsister was a preteen, one of the two boys was an infant and the other little boy was around six or seven years old. And there at the gate was a five-year-old boy who did not come any closer. That little boy also happened to be the son of Umoti Devi's from her second husband Dal bahadur Chherti. His name was Mithun. Everyone told her about her half brother. Maya tried to give him candy, but he would not come to her. Therefore, Maya went up to him and gave him some candies but the kid tried to run away but she caught him. Then he accepted the candies. Then her mother called for Mithun.

Here is the ironic part, Maya is in the same town with a mother she has not seen in seven years. Instead of coming to visit her and greet her, Maya's mother just called out to her son and completely ignored Maya. There is no acknowledgement of her own birth daughter's presence this particular time.

The stepmother with her speech impaired tone asked Maya to stay with them and not to see her mother. Nevertheless, she wanted to meet her mother. Therefore, the next day, at dawn, she sneaked out quietly.

Her mother lived on the same hill as her father but a bit further and higher up on the hills of the village. Her stepfather did offer to take her in but Maya refused to be with strange person she did not know. Her mother and father did talk to one another but lived separately with their new families.

Maya finally met her mother after so many years of separation. It is at this time as an innocent teen who did not know all things at hand she begged her mother to cook her all her favorite foods that she used to have as a child. Surprisingly Mother obliged and cooked everything she loved as a child. Mother and Maya cried. Nevertheless, Mother did not ask her where she had been or about her difficulties.

Apparently Mother only asked her about Kisan and where he was. Maya also did not volunteer any information to her mother about her hardships and torments of the past seven years. Maya basically told her Kisan was in a good, secure place and was happy. She further replied stating that it was her bad luck that she did not get to stay there and study with him while she had a chance. She stayed at her mother's the whole day. In the evening, her stepmother called her and asked her to come back, and she did leave unwillingly. The next morning again, early at dawn she went back to mother's place. Maya did this for quite some time. She left her stepmother's at night when everybody slept and came back before they woke up.

Police men and other messengers were sent to her dad's place of work to let him know that his daughter was now home waiting to see him. At this point in life when you have finally made it this far and are so close to your own father and mother, your feelings are good and you start to think all will be well from this day forward.

Maya though the same thoughts and patiently waited for this moment in anticipation of good things to follow.

For ten days in total she and her uncle stayed at Dad's place waiting, but Dad never came to see her nor did he acknowledge she was there. Feeling the rejection by her own birth father was devastating and humiliating for Maya as she was already brokenhearted after spending seven years in slavery. Her mother also did not want to be around her after that first day's visit. Maya was within the physical comfort of togetherness with her father and mother and now she just found out she was no longer wanted.

Thanks to a good Samaritan Salik Ram, he knew this situation was not in Maya's favor. He was not going to let his brother's mistake be a curse upon him, so he did something about it. Although I never got to see or meet him, he is still my hero for what he did for my sister.

Maya's uncle knew better not to leave her there as she had seen enough trauma already. He realized she would face further difficulties if he left her with either of the families there. After waiting in vain for such a long time, her uncle took her to Tinsukia, Assam where he and his family lived instead.

Tinsukia is situated 480 kilometers (298 mi) northeast of Guwahati and 84 kilometers (52 mi) kilometers away from the border with Arunachal Pradesh. In Tinsukia, Assam at Dad's older brother's house Maya found the refuge she had always longed for. There was love and a sense of being a part of a family again. Maya stayed with her uncle for two years and finally she was married at the age of 17.

Girls are not treated well by their in-laws in Asia, especially in India in the Hindu culture and especially not in a small remote village where women have no value. Each year over 5 million baby girls are aborted in government hospitals. Too many stories are published about how baby girls are killed, and buried alive in India each day. They are the outcasts and rejects of society. This practice most commonly happens in small and remote villages among mostly poor families. Parents worry about finding the money to pay the wedding dowries of daughters. Although demanding dowry has been banned for over 50 years in India it is still a tradition that lives on across all social classes. Many feel that girls place such a burden on their families that some believe it better that they are never born.

Now with technology such as ultrasound scans to determine the sex of the baby parents often pay for an abortion if it is a girl. Some Indians ignore the growing incidents of sex selective abortions. They believe that the girl is better to be killed before the birth rather than after. Luckily, for Maya, she was not aborted during childbirth.

Maya stayed with her uncle's family for two years and he treated her like his own daughter. He had two sons and two daughters. If someone asked who she was, she said she was his eldest daughter. He worked for the railways and lived near the railway colony.

After two years, came a proposal for marriage. An intermediary called Guru Prasad went to Maya's uncle with the proposal. He said the groom was from a fine family and they should go meet him. The uncle's wife went to see them in the Bahadur tea garden. Her uncle also agreed finally but they had one problem: the community there was mostly immigrants from Orissa and Bihar who did labor work and there were very few Nepalese people. Maya's aunt was worried but liked the groom. Everyone assured them it would be fine. Therefore, Maya married Kulprasad Sharma, who was a cook in the estate manager's bungalow.

Maya continued to face difficulties after three to four years of marriage mainly from her in-laws. There were sixteen people in her in-laws' place: five brother-in-laws and four daughter-in-laws. Her husband hardly stayed at home and he mostly lived in the manager's bungalow. Again, Maya had to do all the work.

Whenever her uncle came over to see her, her in-laws fought with him and complained a lot about her and even stopped her from visiting her uncle's place.

Her uncle used to come near her in-laws house and cry. He never went to meet them but just cried and left simply because he was a kindhearted man and was not able to see condition of his daughter's living condition. He mainly blamed himself for giving her up for marriage not knowing that Maya would suffer even more after marriage. Here was another case of greedy, mean in-laws. If the girl's family is too poor to provide such gifts whether it be money, animals or jewelry, accidents happen. There are such accidental deaths of thousands of young woman every year. Some young women end up committing suicide because of such harassment from their "loving" in-laws. Such suicides and burnings, sometimes referred as kitchen accidents or "dowry deaths" are becoming too common.

To maintain their own stature and family morals and values for securing a future daughter-in-law, Maya's in-laws and their entire family went on the offensive by confronting Guru Prasad (the eldest son of her uncle) and accusing him of ruining Maya's life.

Maya's husband was the oldest son. The second son was not married. Her in-laws went searching for a wife. Therefore, they went to her uncle's place to pacify him in case he said something against them to the bride's family. They asked if he knew anyone who wanted to marry off his daughter. Maya did not say anything against them. Maya's uncle said he already had done an injustice to his daughter and made her shed tears and that he did not want to put anyone else through such pain.

He refused Maya's in-laws to help them find a girl, although he did not say anything directly against them. Therefore, the in-laws were offended. They could not find a bride for their second son and he remained single for a long time.

Everytime a girl's family rejected their offer, the in-laws blamed it on Maya and her uncle. They believed they conspired together so that any marriage could be ruined. They harassed her and blamed her for all the failed alliances or any other problems in the household.

Maya's uncle retired and returned to Tinsukia with his elder son, as he did not get his pension. His wife, two daughters and younger son went to Nepal. Around this time, Maya fell seriously sick due to the constant harassment and mental abuse and agony. After this heartbreaking situation with her marriage, Maya once again tried to commit suicide for the second time. So she took a bottle of medicine, not knowing what it was, and went to the fields, hoping to end her life. Nevertheless, her sister-in-law saw her and stopped her in time. Maya's in-law scolded her: she may die but if she did then they will get into trouble and go to jail. They accused her of being evil and wanted them to suffer because of her acts. Maya cried every day.

After some time, her entire body swelled up and became weaker. She could hardly walk but somehow managed to work. Her mother-in-law did not do anything and waited until Maya finished doing her work and cooked the meals.

A driver came everyday to drink water and to listen to the 7 am news on the radio. He frequently visited Maya because of their acquaintance to check up on her to see if she needed anything on a frequent basis. Despites all of her hardships, she was friendly with everyone and most people fell in the love with her the moment they met her. Maya shared her stories with him, especially the ones about her cruel in-laws. One day her sickness became too severe and she could not even get up. The driver came as usual and called for her but no one responded. Her mother-in-law was asleep and never bothered to do anything around the house and she only woke up when the food was prepared. Curious, the driver went inside and saw Maya and he knew Maya was not normally like that. Even if she were sick, she would work. She cried and said that she would not survive. She sweated profusely and her clothes were wet. He shouted at the in-laws. How dare they treat her like that? He would call the police and have them arrested. The driver told Maya's in-laws that he would tell the manager of the tea estate of their abuse and will take away their jobs. The in-laws got scared and they took action on behalf of Maya's life.

Her father-in-law went to the tea estate manager and asked him to help them. He called an ambulance and took her to a new hospital in Rongpuria. She was admitted for one month.

The in-laws thought that if they did not inform her uncle he would blame them so they went to her uncle's place to give him the news but he was not there. They told his neighbors. Then Maya's uncle came back late and was about to have dinner when neighbors told them about Maya. He left dinner sitting on the table and went running to the hospital which he reached at six in the morning. He cried when he saw her all sick and swelled up. Maya laughed and asked him why he was crying and she said she was fine.

He brought food for her every day, for every meal and he asked her if she wanted to eat anything else. Salik Ram her uncle took care of her. Her sickness was so severe that Maya needed blood transfusion which she did not have money for, but he somehow managed to pay for it. Ironically the in-laws came to see her on Sundays, only because it was an off day. They came only to give food. In the midst of Hindu festivities where family members celebrate and spend time with families at home Maya spent Durga puja and Kali puja in the hospital with her uncle. Slowly but surely she recovered and was released after a month's stay.

First she went to her uncle's place and stayed there for a few days. Then she went back to in-laws' house after that. They did not ill-treat or harass her. They left her alone. A few years later Maya gave birth to a daughter, Site Devi. Maya was 21 years old.

Maya got a job as a tea leaves plucker right after marriage and she resumed this job after she came back from hospital. She went to the manager and asked for a new house to live in with her children, away from her in-laws. Her in-laws used to take away all the money she earned. Now she wanted to eat and live separately. However, her husband did not know what went on at home and he did not even know about Maya being hospitalized. After he found out he came home more frequently and finally when they got the new house he lived with her.

The in-laws had a change of heart after Maya's daughter was born. They cooked food for her, took care of her, and gave her warm water to bathe in. She lived well separately from them. Two years later a son was born, Ishwari Prasad. Her father-in-law soon retired and the tea estate manager wanted to give the vacancy to her not to her brother-in-law. Her mother-in-law made a huge fuss, as she wanted the job to be given to her younger son. She harassed Maya saying she had sons who were eligible for the work. The old woman cursed her and accused her of conspiring against the family and that Maya wanted them to suffer. Maya went to the manager and cried and asked for a new job. She did not want the vacancy. He agreed and gave her a new job while her brother-in-law got the vacancy. After a month, her job became permanent.

Two years later her second son, Radhakrishna, was born.

From this time forward, her life somewhat became normal for her even in a poor living condition. Maya began to live a better life. She was happy and content for most part thereafter. Her in-laws, however, suffered a lot simply because of their own attitude and selfishness. None of their children wanted to take care of them and thus all of them left them as they aged. Therefore, the burden of helping them fell on her. Now all of a sudden the role changed as her aged in-laws went to her for help.

After I had finally found my sister and mother, I asked my sister if my aunt who left us on the streets of Kathmandu was still alive. Maya with smirky smile replied that she passed away while I still was in Nepal. Then she inquired to me and asked why I asked about her.

I replied that had she still been alive, I would have made a trip to her village and slapped her for what she did. But for Maya, even after so much heartache, turmoil and so much suffering from her own family and her evil in-laws she found pity on them when they needed her to take care of them. What type of heart, soul and mind does it take to give back such loving care to someone who has just put you through such pain? She really has a big great heart. If you were to open her heart and see the sorrow of yesterdays, it had not even completely healed yet, she has already started the healing of others.

In their old age, the in-laws returned her love and started praising her instead of harassing her. They also sent folks to Maya to tell her that they always supported her and never meant to give her a hard time. People came and told Maya all these things and she did not say anything bad about the in-laws to them, as they were now frail and already suffering a lot. She thought it was better to just keep quiet and let things be.

Where was her mom or dad all this time? Why were they not looking for her or even inquiring about her? Her dad knew very well who she was with last. Why did he not attempt to find her again? The question will remain unanswered forever.

From Tinsukia, Assam to Nepalgunj, Nepal after years of struggle, Maya looked up to see her dad's older brother staring at her. He was a God-sent angel to her because he came looking for both kids that was separated at early age.

Maya had been working in the Bahadur Tea Estate in her town at a hospital built to care for all laborers who work at the tea estate. Bahadur Tea Estate has been kind to her and all the workers. All the employees of the estate are given free quarters to live in as long as they are employed there. Although very little salary is given to the staff, their health care, housing and vacation every year is provided free of charge.

Although Maya is only three years older than me, she appeared much older simply because of the harsh and rough life she had been through. At the hospital, Maya worked with sick patients and cared for them and they all loved her. She served food to sick patients and sometimes fed them if they are too sick as well. Isn't it interesting that we both gravitated to nursing? Maya seemed to be a very cheerful woman despite the fact she has gone through hell on earth already. At home Maya kept herself busy looking after the little possessions she had such as chickens, roosters and goats.

She cooked and cared for her gentle husband and three children. Maya's husband also works at the tea estate, cooks for the estate director, and has been employed there forever.

My sister is always positive and loved to hear me call her "Sani" like I used to when were kids. The short time I did get to visit and be with her, she always smiled and said how grateful she is for being able to see her brother's face and talk to him after all of these years of separation. After a great visit with my sister and her family, it was soon time to say goodbye again. With tears in both of our eyes, I jokingly told her, you left me when I was a kid and you are getting ready to leave again.

She cried but it was not the same cries as it was when she said goodbye to me long ago in Nepal. It was a cry of joy knowing that I was OK and we now became family again. I have always been close to my sister ever since we were on the streets. We cried, we smiled, we starved but we both survived. She took care of me and looked after me not just as a young brother, but as a mother as well. She will always remain in my heart forever until death do us part. I'd like to dedicate this poem in honor of my courageous sister who I love so much.

Maya now

For my sister Sani:
Thank you sister for your love and care,
I hope that you continue my new prayer.
Hope you remain my only sister forever,
For that I will make it my daily prayer.

May God give you wisdom and grace,
Hope we never end up in the same place. you fed me, cared and
loved me as child, though you yelled at me, but mostly smiled.
although our childhood memories haunt us both, let our past be
our everlasting growth.
As you were just a child yet became my mom,
That is the reason I now sing a psalm.

I shall cherish your love forever and ever,
As share your love to whomsoever.
You gave shelter, cared for my life, healed the scar left behind by
family strife.

You begged with strangers so that I would be fed, knowing well of
each other's common need.
Thank you and I love you is all I have to say,
Now that we found each other, let us not betray.

Forty years was long enough for me to wait,
I will love you forever which words can't translate.
Thank you being there when I needed you the most, now and
forever I hope we stay very close.

CHAPTER 9
The Story Of Umoti Devi (My Mom, The Last 40 Years Without Her Kids)

Umoti Devi (known by me and my sister Maya, as Mote Devi). Her real name on the passport indicates her name as being Uma Devi, born March 3rd, 1943. My birth mother left us when I was about four years old and my sister Maya was about eight years old. Mom said she did not leave us because she did not care for us. Life's harsh circumstances in the Hindu country of India and the marriage problem and abuse by her husband forced her to leave behind two wonderful loving kids she adored. She claims that her (my dad) husband had multiple wives but I never saw any of them as a child.

I do not know much about this but I felt that she loved me as a child until the day she walked away leaving me and my sister behind. I remembered her and thought about her all the time from early childhood and even to this day. I wonder did she remember me?

Well 40 plus years have passed since she gave me that last orange. When I saw her face-to-face on live TV I found out that she still loved me and that she did come looking for me—at least that is what she said. She does claim that she searched the streets of Kathmandu for three straight days until what little money she had was depleted. She did not have any money and was poor so she could not continue with the search. I could have been at the orphanage not far from where she was searching for me. I do not think she knew that my sister had already returned to our aunt's place and was living somewhere in Nepalgunj. Had she gone to our aunt's house, she could have found both of us but I do not think she realized that both my sister and I at that time were in two completely different locations by then.

There was a character that we used to call uncle as children and we nicknamed him Junge Mama, (junja meaning person with a big and long mustache). He used to live with us and worked odd jobs around the house while we were with my parents. His name was Dal Bahadur Chhetri. Dal Bahadur Chhetri was around all the time while our father was away from home. I think he had seen the abuse first hand and perhaps asked our mother to leave Dad and to settle with him during that time. After mother took off, so did Dal Bahadur.

Unexpectedly our aunt showed up looking for her younger brother, my dad, and asked my dad and the entire family to move to Nepal. She offered to take the entire family to her home in Nepalgunj and take care of us. Mom even agreed to go that time but dad with his current job situation said to take the rest of the family and he would join us later. The day prior to our departure day, Mom ran away. Dad sent me and my sister with our aunt to Nepalgunj. Months go by and he does not show up nor sends any money for us. Six months later mother gets married to our so-called uncle who lived with us and starts a new life with Dal Bahadur Chhetri.

There's an ironic twist to this story in that Mom must have really loved Dad though he was abusive to her because a few months after she got remarried, she felt sorry for Dad and introduced him up with another woman. They got married in 1971 shortly thereafter. She did not feel like he should live alone and found a young poor woman who was dumb, so to speak. She had a speech disorder and was slow.

But while she was remarried and started a new relationship with Dal Bahadur our so called uncle, she showed up at my dad's house to inquire about us. Where are my kids and what did you do to them? A fight broke out and he blamed her for leaving him and she blamed him for the abuse. She kept haunting him about us but Dad just ignored her. Dad on the other hand blamed her for seeing Dal Bahadur Chettri who was a helper at the house and did odd jobs and who supposedly had a crush on my mom and showed more love to her than my father. With someone willing to take care of her more than my dad, she took off with him.

Not married to her new lover, but living with him, she came back to my dad to confront him about us again. Dad just blamed her for leaving her kids because of her love affairs and giving up her kids to be with someone else. The fight went on but it did not reach any conclusion for either one to come and start looking for us.

Mother finally married this guy and started a new life. My sister and I are out of the picture by now since she had her own son with our "uncle."

My mother's story remained the same as the one she told on live TV, which didn't make me impressed with her story of abandoning me and my sister. So once I returned back to the States and started investigating I called my other relatives. I also learned that I have many other half brothers and sisters whom I have never met. I was not quite done with just finding my mom and sister at all. My quest to now reunite with our remaining other family members was my next priority. I challenged myself and talked to my wife and decided that I am going to inquire and find my extended family. One by one I collected each and every member of my family including my only surviving great aunt Khagisara, along with her deceased husband (my uncle) and her oldest son Guru who was responsible for coming to look for me and my sister. Now that I have rest of the family members' contact information, I called each and every one and asked them to meet me at one central location in Nawalparasi district of Nepal where most of my other relatives were living. On March 14th, 2012, I travelled to Nepal to meet the rest of my family members.

It was at this time I learned that my mom was not being honest with me and was not telling even today the real reason why she actually took off leaving two kids behind.

Sadly I learned that the so-called uncle was her lover due to the fact that Dad was almost always gone and when he did come home he was abusive towards her. This uncle or Dal Bahadur was the only one she spent most of her time with while Dad was working during the weekdays and us kids were at school. Dal Bahadur and Mom had built a relationship to a point where he showed her love and affection that she could not resist. Thus in order to avoid being abused she ran away with him leaving us both behind. Not too long after she was remarried she had a child named Mithu, my half brother. Mom and her newlywed husband then started a wine making business and sold wines to customers. Mom remained in the same general area where my father lived. Her successful business had started catering to mostly the police officers nearby my father's police station. There she was making a good living and was happy with her new life and husband who actually treated her very well and cared for like woman should be treated.

During the course of starting the wine shop and making good living, Mother was mistreated by one of the customers. My mom as I have come to know her now is cunning and sharper than a two-edged sword. She is fast to respond and quick to answer. It is her way or the highway. She is smart for her age even now. So smart that she does not realize her words and things she says are hurting her relationship with her newly found long lost son and daughter. Not to mention all other relatives of hers.

Well it is at her new bar that a police constable became a regular visitor. He started to flirt and started use some filthy language with my mother. My mom must be temperamental judging by her attitude and the things she says versus what she does. She was not a typical Nepalese young lady who will take the slander from just about anyone. The culture for men and woman is different in a small remote village in India. Women are treated badly by men and even by their own parents. Normally they would bow down and take whatever abuse comes their way. Especially the abuse from their husband, but once she remarried, perhaps she had change in attitude to fight for her rights. She was not going to let anyone get away with giving her a hard time anymore. As this customer was semi-high ranking officer who started to give her hard time at her own home bar, my mother took a Khukari Gorkha Army knife and meant to beat or hit this man with the back of the blade, but she accidental hit him on his shoulder with the blade side and cut his arm off. The sounds of extreme pain and agony gathered the villagers and soon my mom was escorted to jail. It was her young son Mithu, at about age four, who cared and walked miles to take food to his mother as she spent many months in jail until bond was set for her to come out.

Once she got out of jail then her current husband was taken into custody. Later with a bail bond he was temporarily released from jail and that is when mom, my stepfather and half brother Mithu packed by night and boarded a train and vanished into thin air and ended up in Nepal. Out of fear, she and her hubby packed up and ran away to Kavry district in Nepal. Kavry is a picturesque village situated northwest of Kathmandu valley. It is a fairly remote village where no transportation is available at all. In order to get there, one must take a day's journey by bus and you must hike for six hours on foot. There are fantastic views of the Himalayas and agriculture is the main job for most people. She lived there for at least ten years or so until her second husband passed away. After that, she once again moved to Assam, India and lived with Bal Ram Sharma, her adopted younger brother.

In Hindu tradition there is a festival called Bhai tika, which is the last day of Diwali celebrations in Nepal and in some parts of India. It is the most important day and is known as Bhai tihar. On this brother and sister day, the sister prays to Yamraja for her brother's long life and prosperity. The royal astrologer gives the appropriate time to apply the tika on the forehead through the national radio a day before and the entire nation abides by it. Even his majesty, the king of Nepal receives tika from his sisters. When his majesty receives tika a thirty-one-gun salute is given to honor the function. At this moment, the entire nation will be observing Bhai Tika.

Legend holds that when the Kirat king fell ill, Yama sent messages in the form of dogs and crows. At this time, Bali Hang's sister guarded him by sending messages that he could take only after fulfilling certain conditions; that the god of death should wait till Panchami, i.e. Bhai tika. She also put forth conditions that Yama should not take Bali Hang until the tika, which she had smeared on his forehead, fades away, the sprinkled water dries and the makhmali (a kind of flower) flower wilts. The main intention behind Bhai Tika is for the sisters to pray for their brother's long life from Yama Raj, god of the underworld.

With that said, my mother did not have a younger brother and had to honor a younger brother since she was a Hindu woman. She was asked by a close relative to adopt a young kid by the name of Bal Ram Sharma who was about six years older than me to be her god brother for life.

Currently in Nepal, she lives in the remote mountain. She somehow managed to open up a small tea/coffee shop to keep her and her family sustained. She raised her son from her second marriage in that village but also managed to put her son through school up to the 6th grade. According to my mom after my initial reunion she told me that Mithu her own son later managed to sell all of her land and managed to transfer all her properties and land in his name and never told her about it. He even took her original birth certificate and managed to leave her the photocopy with her.

As I finished my second tour to visit the rest of my relatives including my half brother Mithu, I am alarmed with the fact that my mother is nothing but a habitual liar and cunning woman. Once her second husband passed away, she braved it again and returned to Assam, India to be with her adopted brother Bal Ram and later moved to Nagaland, bordering India.

She stayed at Bal Ram Sharm's home for four to six years. While there, she cared for Bal Ram's son who was just a child at the time. There's a story that she often cared for the young kid named Arjun and pretended he was me and she adored him as if he was her own son Kisan. However, nonetheless she made no effort to look for me other than once she came to Kathmandu for three days and gave up. Not to mention I was perhaps only 4 kilometers (2.5) miles away from the place where she came to search for me.

While she was still with her brother in India she met yet another man, Gopal Gurung. As she spent more and more time with Gopal, she would spend many nights out. Her brother came looking for her and asked her to come home but she would make all kinds of excuses not to go home with him just so that she could spend some time with her new found love at her old age. Not being able to talk her into coming home Bal Ram and Mom exchanged words in such a way that Bal Ram basically gave up and they quit talking to each other for a long time. Later she managed to get married to yet a third husband and moved her young son back to Nepal with her new husband and got her son Mithu at the age of 11 to marry an educated girl from whom five kids were born. Once the oldest married and had a grand baby, Umoti Devi became a great grandma now. Her daughter-in-law hated Mom so much that she even told her that when she dies that she would kill a fat goat weighing up to 40-kilos and have feast when she passed away.

What a family life to live in such a hatred environment! I did not want to go into details as to why the daughter-in-law hated her so much. My half-brother volunteered the fact that he had four girls and one son and mom tried to starve one of the youngest daughters to death. As I mentioned earlier in the book, girls are unwanted in Hindu society for various reasons, especially when there are too many girls in the family. During the grand reunion she spoke with a soft voice that she was not loved and was afraid of her grandma during her childhood.

She said that they had a puppy at their house when she was little. She took shelter with the puppy and would sleep next to the puppy who at least showed her love more than a human being. My brother Mithu was just a kid himself when he started to have kids. How was he supposed to back talk to Mom and tell her no to such harsh conditions? Being a young newlywed and mistreated probably had a lot to do with how my brother's wife wanted to celebrate the death of my mom or least it appears that way. It was the same situation as with my own sister. My sister suffered a great deal during her marriage while her in-laws were alive. Personally my in-laws in the west are very loving and caring despite that I have married into a interracial marriage.

For Asian people, the Hindu religion and culture that dictates how society should be, I am dumfounded with the fact these types of injustices ever exist.

While she hated her daughter in-law and the many kids, she loved her son. After the events of first reunion unfolded, I was in the process of trying to get her a passport to bring her to the States. I was thrilled to find Mom after so many years. She was brought to my friend's Deepak's house in Chitawan city, I had asked her to return to Kathmandu and get her passport ready but she made a trip to see her son in the west to settle unfinished business first. Three days later, she showed back at my friend Deepak's house with her son from her second marriage. We chatted for the first time via Skype and I was able to see his face for about five minutes. Since then he called me once and that was the end of it for a while until I get a sudden phone call from him again.

He even went out and got himself a computer so that he can communicate me via Skype or email now. I hope to continue to keep the dialog open and find out more family details.

So every now and then, Mithu calls me via Skype and we see each other face-to-face and have chats online. Now that he has access to the internet and has figured out how to use Skype through his older son, he keeps in touch with me on a regular basis. I have also had to remotely teach one of his young teenage daughters how to open a Yahoo email so that she can chat with me via email. Technology has thus help me with communicating and reuniting me with my immediate and extended family.

For some unknown reasons the third man in her life took my mother to his ancestral place on the hills of the Sindhupalchok district in the Northern Himalayas of Kathmandu, Nepal. This is where she is currently living with her third husband.

As an adult looking back I can now understand the disappointments that made my mother the woman she became. Nonetheless, she did manage to go through life without emotional melodrama after being ill treated by her own husband.

On Mother's Day this year I called her and simply asked her how she was. She said fine. At this time I had not called her in two weeks' time. She said she was worried why I had not phoned her in such a long time. I was out of town on a training assignment, therefore I was unable to call her as frequently as I wanted. She was content with my answer. I went on to tell her, "Happy Mother's Day" but had to explain to her that May 13th was Mother's Day in the U.S. It was the day that we honor our mothers and do something nice for them. I told her that I was grateful that I was able to call her on Mother's Day and wish her a happy Mother's Day for the first time in my life. She paused and said she was happy to hear my voice and to know I am still alive.

Our conversation was short due to the fact she is not hearing very well and long distance calls keep dropping in the remote village of Nepal. Nonetheless it made her day to hear my voice and to receive a call from me. She basically asked how her grandchildren and my wife were doing. I gave her the good news that all of us are doing well, and she just said please keep calling her at least once a week and she would like to hear from me more often.

It is not easy for a child to be without a mother nor father, yet during this great journey of my life, I found many mothers and fathers as I grew up. Yes, there was no Mother's Day for me nor were there any hugs and kisses from my mother, but I found lots of hugs and kisses from others who became my mother. Much as I regret those hard days of my childhood without her, I never once regretted what happened to me and my sister. It was what my life was meant to be. Had it not been for God's perfect will, I would not be where I am now. With some disappointments yet with love I like to dedicate this poem to my dearest mother that I finally found.

As we've been drowning in tears for many years
The kids you abandoned with no fears
We may never know what you were thinking
With newfound love you were greatly adapting
Did you ever try to look back with regret?
But I looked for you without being upset.
Many years has passed, but I never gave up
Though not easy I would find you soon enough

Finally through friends and the internet
And Facebook, I was able to connect
With someone who cares enough
I found some clues about the real stuff

Why were you not there when I needed you the most?
The one and only that I could trust,
Time may heal the scars you left behind. Finding you again gives
me peace of mind.

As my desire to find you became imminent
A lifelong burden became an accomplishment
Meeting you after so long was a joyous moment no doubt
But knowing my father had passed away was a dark cloud
I had many things that I wanted to ask him
I guess chances of finding the answers far too dim

But at least my sister and I have come to you still alive
We hope and pray that you don't let us deprive
We will still love you no matter what has been done
I hope you still love us both in the long run.

CHAPTER 10

My Dad's Story

Dad

My dad was Indra Lal Upadhaya, the youngest of three sons of my grandfather Nandal Lal Upadhaya. He was also married off at a young age. He was just a teen when he got married to my mom when my mom was only nine years old and his parents moved to Assam, India for a better job. His dad Nandalal arranged the marriage and helped him move to India. After being in India for many years, he asked his dad to find him a wife not knowing he was already married and his wife was in the Parbat district of Nepal. It is when his dad got mad at him and went back to Nepal and brought his wife, my mother, along with his older brother's wife who was also left behind back to India and they settled there in Kahilipara, India. This is where my sister and I were born according to my mom. I do remember the brief comforts of my home with my mother and father which was short lived. My sister and I did not get to enjoy much time with our dad due to the fact he was gone during weekdays and only home on the weekends.

Growing up I never talked about him to anyone but a single friend that there was no one in my life that I could call "Dad." I personally did not get to know him as much as I wanted and never did get to know him after I was separated from him at age four.

After the constant abuse my mother took off and left Dad to fend for himself, leaving two kids behind. A few days later, our aunt shows up at our house. Dad was working in remote site where he would be gone during the week and came home only during the weekends. With no one to look after the kids during his absence, he instructed our aunt to take the kids away from him to remote area of Nepal where our grandparents lived. Now he was a free man with no kids and no worries; he never wondered where his kids were and what they were doing. While my sister and I were struggling to make sense of what was going on, amidst of all chaos,

Dad remarried and settled down with his newly married wife. In the beginning of my story I mentioned that my daddy loved me and we were happy little family. As I have come to know my dad now who is no longer with us, I have also come to find out that he really was not a great dad after all. Today, yesterday's "good father" has retroactively become an emotionally distant, uncaring villain. The father who supposed to be the bread winner for the family is seen as selfish and not loving at all.

After my second reunion with my entire family, I got the details about my dad from his second wife and my half brother and sisters from dad's second marriage. My dad married a young lady who is virtually deaf. She cannot hear what others say, however, she can speak very well. I suppose she can hear despite what others say. I spoke to her and got answers from her when I visited her home and her village during my grand reunion with entire family and other relatives.

The same story of abuse echoed from all members of the family including my great aunt who knew him well. Being deaf, hard of hearing and uneducated, his second wife was just as badly abused by my father as my mother was or perhaps even worse.

My half brother and half sister I talk to from Dad's side give me no indications of love towards them. How could he have had an additional three children when he could not even find in his heart to come searching for me and my sister in first place?

I chatted with my half brother and sister trying to find out how life was for them with their dad but all conversations end with same sad story as he kept drinking and he used to abuse their mom as well.

Then I asked them how about their relationship with Dad, and they shared the same old story that he never was home and whenever he was home a fight broke out between Mom and Dad. Normally it was one sided fight with the kids caught up in the mess.

My dad remarried in 1973. Before starting his second family, he would just do his own thing of coming home and minding his business and going to work again for weeks. But once he was remarried, he continued to work and took an early retirement few years later. At what age did he retire I do not have any idea but it was after the third son Raju was born. He ended up having three kids from the second marriage.

Here are my half brother and half sisters along with their ages:
Pabitra Sharma, my half sister Age 38
Ram Prasad Sharma half brother age 35
Raja Sharma half brother 28

But with his second family he resorted to drinking even more than before. I don't know whether he missed his kids and a wife or just because. If he did miss his kids why he never came looking for them is beyond my imagination. Did he miss his wife? I don't know that either. But from listening to relatives who know him well say that he resorted to heavy drinking because of him losing his kids and his wife. Does not make any sense to me but that is what I was told. He got so upset about something in his life that he even had a car accident that almost killed him. Neighbors, friends and family members asked him to slow down and stop abusing his body with alcohol, but he never listened to anyone. He got so out of control that the police department had to demote him from his constable general position to just constable.

He was not himself and never once said goodbye or even said I love you kids when he left for his duty. While all these things are going on his own family members begged him to go looking for his two first-born kids and he kept making promises to go searching for them but he never did. Dad was just like before; he was always gone because he was stationed at the border of Assam and Bangladesh and he only came home during weekends. He kept his old habit and was mostly abusive even to his second wife according to his middle son Ram Prasad Sharma who now lives in southern part of Nepal in a town called Daldale.

The girls did admit he loved their mom but the boys were scared of him. My brother Ram went on to tell me that he spent his weekends at his friend's house by daytime and came home and slept beside Dad after he had fallen asleep. He did not want to face Dad during the time he was home and awake. My stepmom is a devout Hindu whom I tried to show her how to worship above and not below on the ground as she does not hear or understand a word others say. But she just smiled back at me and hugged me with the love and affection as though she knew me as the oldest son. She treated me well and I felt loved. Much more so than my own mother who was also with me. My mother would not even hug and kiss my forehead while my stepmom hugged and kissed me with admiration.

She is a very clean and neat woman. She tells her kids that they should not wear same clothes more than once until it is washed. Makes sure they shower daily and she keeps the hut clean. She wakes up early and makes sure the house is clean while the grown up kids and grandkids are still asleep. She performs her Hindu rituals as most religious people do. She tries to talk and laugh as I am talking to other members of the family and pretends to have heard and understood everything despite her disability.

She suffered a great deal during her marriage but managed to raise my three siblings with what little she had. Dad never gave her any money to take care of the kids. She sold firewood and milked cow and goat's milk to raise the kids that are now all grown. What a great woman and a great mother she has been to all of her three kids who are all now married.

My great aunt Kashihgara when inquired about the situation, blamed both my mom and dad for the tragic situation that took place. She never envisioned that a mother and father could do such a thing to their children. I was able to chat with her over the phone briefly and she cried and said she loved me and my sister. She said that it was her and her husband who actually stood up and said, if our father did not care, they would go looking for us. They found my sister but not me. I was told that he passed away around 1996, which would have been 9 years after I came to U.S.

Judging from the fact that he never inquired about my sister, or me I get the feeling he did not care about his kids. That thought was confirmed when my sister was 15 and dad's older brother rescued her. Maya was brought back to the Kahilipara village in Guwahati. A message was sent to our Dad to come visit his daughter but he never attempted to come. My sister waited with her uncle at Dad's residence for over 12 days but there was no sign of Dad or any acknowledgement from dad that he was or was not coming.

Very little is known of my dad's side of the story. I may never know the truth ever since I never got a chance to see him alive. I only have very vague memories of him simply because I was only four years when my life with my father ended forever. What little memories of my father, I was grateful to finally see a photo.

From his second marriage came three kids now all grown and settled. One of my half sisters, Pabitra from dad's second marriage is still in Assam, India. She saw me on live TV more than 10 times and heard the entire story. I am dumfounded as to why she never made an effort to contact me while I was still in India during that time. Two months later I did get a chance to speak with her but never bothered to ask her why she did not try to make any contact either. My other half brother who was in Nepal at the time had no idea what was going on with me and the current chain of events that was taking over my life. Once I made the contact with my half sister in India, then only did she call her brother and tell him the story. Immediately after receiving the call and getting my cell number, he made an attempt to contact me from Nepal. Not knowing the number and not having a Caller ID, I ignored the phone calls for two weeks. Finally he was able to catch up to me two months after the fact and phoned me.

The youngest of my half brothers, Raju was in Middle East working to support his own family in Nepal. He has since then returned back home to Nepal and planning to go back later. I personally have not seen him or met him yet. He is now aware of the recent developments and we have yet to chat with each other and catch up on our stories. I was not aware of the fact that my two uncles from my dad's side had passed away but I found my aunt who was still alive and well in southern part of Nepal. I also managed to locate my stepmother through my friend Deepak who happens to live only 25 kilometer from my relatives. Once I received a phone call from my half brother, I phoned Deepak to go visit them and get some answers. Deepak has been a detective and journalist for me from the beginning of my search. It was not a case of divorce that caused us to suffer; it was the negligence from two grown adults who left us scared forever.

Upon finding my extended family, they all have requested that I come along with my older sister to Nepal for a grand reunion sometime soon. I have promised in God's time when I can find the resources to take my family, I would try to fulfill their quest to see me especially my great aunt who is of an advanced age and is not feeling all that well. She mentioned that she would like to see me before she passes away. I hope and pray that God would pave the way for me to get there before she passes away.

THE GRAND REUNION

Once the dust had settled after finding my mother and elder sister, I did not stop there either. I knew that my mother and father was remarried and had other siblings as well. I once again sought help from my friend Deepak and started to question my uncle Bal Ram for finding my other family members. I was told that most of my other half brothers and sister, along with my great aunt lived close to my friend Deepak in Daldaley, a small town near the Indo Nepal border. After I had returned to the U.S., I slowly made connections with the rest of my siblings along with my stepmom. I decided to go meet them all under one roof for the very first time in my life. I had my friend Deepak call each and every one of my relatives and asked them to come visit me in Chitawan, Nepal in March 2012. It was going to be the first ever grand reunion with my entire family including my mom who already in Nepal at this time. I had my half sister and full sister be escorted by my eldest nephew to come to Nepal as well. I made the trip to Nepal to meet with rest of my siblings, step mom, niece and nephews, uncle and aunts and many other family members, including my biological mom who was present. We shared each others' good and bad stories and cried as tears of joys and happiness were conjoined together with many emotions. The life struggle of childhood stories and abandonments and setbacks by parents and spousal abuse of all types were shared. Yet after spending five straight days and chatting we never finished what I wanted to finish during my grand reunion.

Extended family

I spent time one-on-one with my great aunt who cried day after day every time I talk to her. Memories of the past not only haunted me but I could see it in her eyes that it bothered her even now as she is getting close to 70 years in age. Two days after I returned in the U.S., she phoned me to tell me that she misses seeing and talking to me and asked when will I be back?

Memories of the past seem to emerge even today for me yet I never knew what God might have in life for me. Forty years I have asked God to please let me find my family before I die, and here I am united not only with my biological mother and elder sister that I love so much, but with so many half brothers and sisters too. Not to mention uncles and aunts, nieces to nephews and so many cousins; I don't even know each of their names and have not quite comprehended who is who in my life yet. God has been great in my life more than I can fathom.

There are many reasons why parents abandon their children in many countries around the globe. Some youth abandoned by their parents are forced to fend for themselves. Sometimes violence and neglect in a family causes kids to resort to the streets for a better option than to endure what goes on in their own family. Mine was such a case of physical abuse by my father that drove or forced my mother to abandon me at the tender age of four.

As you know there are serious consequences. Recent studies have found when the father is absent in his kids' life, the kids are likely to commit suicide or use drugs, end up in prison as it was in the movie *Courageous* (2011), which I have watched twice. My sister did try to commit suicide twice. When you experience physical trauma and emotion as a child, the wounds might heal up but the scars remain.

This was the case for my elder sister who felt the painful experience of abandonment that exposed a layer of hurt that needed so much healing. It is why even after our reunion where my sister and mother met together for the first time, after all these years, Maya could not look at my mother eye-to-eye for what had transpired in the past. I as an adult tried to make that connection with my lost sister and we hit it off well with the same love, affection and trust we had for each other during our childhood.

Now we have without any reservations reestablished that connection of brother and sisterly love and have restored our relationship back to where we left it long ago. For now and forever everyday is Bhai Tika for me and my sister. I wish I could say the same for my sister and mother's case was the same but it will be a challenge for them.

Since the reunion I have made it possible to have my mother move in with my sister for a few months to mend and rebuild mother/daughter relationship and thus I'm happy to inform you that as of December 24, 2011, my mom now is staying with my sister and is spending quality time with her and her three grandchildren which she had never met before. Praise God for what has happened thus far. Not to mention that my pastor friend also preached and told my mother about Christ and what He means to her prior to her departing Nepal to go spend some with my elder sister.

As for me, I will never forget my time of trial as a young child on the streets of Kathmandu that followed my last orange, but I wish to move past these painful memories so they don't take over my life with loathing and bitterness.

I have learned that carrying grudges and bitterness from the past is not the right medication to let the wounds heal. My scars may remain forever but I choose God's love. In all of my living, God was working His great wonders beyond my imagination to make me who I am today.

From the lessons learned from my own dad I hope to be a better father to my two wonderful kids and raise them in a godly and loving home.

With many difficulties and a determined heart, I made an earnest effort to look for my loved ones. With the right person, right connections, perfect timing and power of technology, I was reunited with my entire family in a fairytale-type live reunion on television in India September 4, 2011. Forty years of desperate searching came to an end with me seeing my biological sister and my mother for the first time, feeling their emotional embrace and tasting tears of joy.

I have since started to track and draw up my family tree or root as you may with all my relatives and their contact information. I had promised myself to keep in touch and continue to do what I can to help and assist them in any way possible. May God Almighty give me the knowledge and wisdom to accomplish what I have promised myself to accomplish in the near future. Among many other things, I have yet to share the joys of what Christ means to me with my long lost family members. I hope it is not too late for me to share the joys and happiness of being a born again Christian with my family so they too may experience what joy I have within me now.

Source:
http://www.thehoot.org/web/home/story.php?storyid=5452&mod=1&pg=1&sectionId=14

In a rather 'film' style, the channel News Live aired my emotional reunion between a mother and her son and daughter after 40 long years. In addition, the story, they claimed, had created television history as it involved three countries—USA (where the long-lost son resides), India (Assam) where the sister was discovered and of course where the television channel is aired from and Nepal (where the mother was discovered and where they had initially lost each other). It was a thrilling moment for all viewers as they could see visuals from two different countries on Skype apart from the scenes from India.

The story began when two officials of Assam police, Rajen Singh and Pranabjyoti Goswami discovered through a Facebook friend in Nepal about another friend, Kisan Upadhaya (currently based in Durham, USA). I am currently an IT professional based in the USA had been desperately trying to look for my mother. I sought these police officials to look for her as my father was also in the Assam police. These police officials managed to track my deceased father, Indralal Upadhaya, who was a constable with the Assam police. They tracked a couple who were my neighbors who knew of me when I was just two and half years old. They appeared on live TV and gave clues about my mother and sister.

Rajen Singh said, "The response to the show has been tremendous. Overnight mine as well as my friends list on face book had increased manifold." The animated show was hosted by the Managing Editor of the channel Syed Zarir Hussain who acted the Sutradhar. Gradually, my poignant tale fell into place. As my mother had abandoned her children and husband and was last seen in Assam's Karbi Anglong district. Me and my elder sister were taken to Nepal by our aunt. There we had a tough time. My sister Maya Devi alias Sani worked as a domestic house cleaner whereas I at five-years-old worked at a Tea Stall and then fell ill and was hospitalized. In addition, for a while I had to even beg on the streets of Kathmandu. Since no one came forward to claim me as their own, I was then taken to an orphanage and this was the time I lost touch with my only sister as well. I had just started my junior year in Nepal's Tribhuvan University. That is when God worked yet another miracle in my life and I was sponsored by Dr. Frank and Ellen Starmer to come to Chapel Hill, North Carolina and attend college in the USA. I however could not forget my mother, father and my sister who I had last seen when I was just five years old. The suspense-packed story, which ran into several episodes, had another aunt and cousin pitching in their bit.

Finally, my elder sister was tracked in Bahadur Tea Estate in Assam's Tinsukia district. One episode comprised of the emotional reunion of me with my elder sister. Television audiences watched spell-bound as the brother and sister met online after 40 long years. I had just woke up and was preparing breakfast. I told the audience that I was excited and highly emotional. I spoke to my sister in Nepalese language for the first time in 40 years addressing her as 'Didi' (meaning elder sister in Nepalese language). My maternal aunt was there in the studio as well to testify that she was indeed the long-lost sister.

My sister asked me to, "Show her the dimple on my cheek." In addition, which I did! The host Hussain asked my sister if she had any doubts if I was her brother. My sister said she was convinced that I was indeed her long-lost brother. In addition, she narrated the traumatic times they we faced in Nepal after our mother had left us. "It's God's wish. I cannot believe it. I quietly prayed for him all these years though I never physically tried to search for him." She did say that her mother came to meet her some 25 years back after she had got married. She said her mother's name is Umoti Devi. Things unfolded dramatically and Umoti Devi was discovered in the next episode at a remote place in Nepal. One of their correspondents was bringing her back to Kathmandu. Then it was the grand moment—a triangular reunion between the mother, son and daughter. Maya, when asked to express her feelings said, "It will be the happiest moment of my life.

My children always asked about their grandmother and uncle. Now they will see them live." Maya also added, "I met my mother some 25 years back. Therefore, I distinctly remember her face. I am confident that I will recognize her." Then came the rather blurred image of Umoti Devi on screen live from Kathmandu due to the low bandwidth. Umoti Devi my mother was seen wiping her tears and the three of us spoke to each other for the first time. Umoti says, "How can I forget the face of my own son and daughter? I want to be close to my son. I had tried to look for him on several occasions. Now I want to go with him." She also narrated why she left them. Her husband Indralal had two wives earlier and she could not tolerate this fact. Then my mother asked to see her daughter-in-law Pam online.

I promised to get my visa and paperwork done as soon as possible and come to meet my mother and sister. Thus ended the seven-day saga on television, which Kisan described as a 'fairytale ending' and a 'movie coming to life'. Thanks to technology, face book and reality television!

Moreover, I thank my God Jesus Christ who said I will never leave nor forsake the. Hebrews 13:5. I am thus God's child and no longer an orphan nor a street kid. As God had his hands in my care from various people who came into my life, my loving wife and I went to Nepal and decided to adopt an orphan girl and to be a blessing on one child. I am unable to help the entire world but was able to rescue one.

I thank all parties mentioned in this book for playing a vital role and lending a helping hands in order to fulfill my quest and life's journey to reunite with my family. Thank you.

From press release in India.

Press releases: Asia and Australia

http://imagechannels.com/tv/video/1320

http://nepaliradio.org/2012/06/kisanupadhyayalife

http://indianherald.com.au/epaper/apr2012/index.htmlPage37-38

http://www1.m.timesofindia.com/PDATOI/
articleshow/9663539.cms

http://www.deccanherald.com/content/184800/separated-40-
years-ago-united.html

http://thehoot.org/web/home/story.php?storyid=5452&mod=1
&pg=1&sectionId=14&valid=true

http://www.dnaindia.com/india/report_separated-40-years-ago-
family-reunites-through-live-tv_1577660

http://www.inewsone.com/2011/08/19/separated-40-years-
ago-united-on-live-tv/69908

US Local news:

http://www.wral.com/news/local/story/10164801/

2012 grand family reunion videos

http://www.firstpost.com/topic/place/nepal-kisan-news-live-
grand-reunion-video-PPHJRVW74yQ-1248-1.html

http://www.youtube.com/watch?v=u8GjW_0Wvdg http://www.youtube.com/watch?v=aDX5R0EFCK8 http://www.youtube.com/watch?v=FWnAIROKvwQ

2011 live TV re-union with mom and sister

http://www.youtube.com/watch?v=Aao2Xtcivbk

http://www.youtube.com/watch?v=2QCaPtRq6tw

http://www.youtube.com/watch?v=fYJPPhnJK7o

http://www.youtube.com/watch?v=aatfl0jruZ4